WHEN IS DADDY
COMING?

WHEN IS DADDY
COMING?

Dealing with Absent
Fatherhood Day by Day

OFELIA PEREZ

ARCHWAY
PUBLISHING

Archway Publishing books may be ordered through booksellers or by contacting:

Archway Publishing
1663 Liberty Drive
Bloomington, IN 47403
www.archwaypublishing.com
1 (888) 242-5904

Because of the dynamic nature of the Internet, any web addresses or
links contained in this book may have changed since publication and
may no longer be valid. The views expressed in this work are solely those
of the author and do not necessarily reflect the views of the publisher,
and the publisher hereby disclaims any responsibility for them.

Any people depicted in stock imagery provided by Thinkstock are models,
and such images are being used for illustrative purposes only.
Certain stock imagery © Thinkstock.

ISBN: 978-1-4808-3505-4 (sc)
ISBN: 978-1-4808-3506-1 (e)

Library of Congress Control Number: 2016912092

Print information available on the last page.

Archway Publishing rev. date: 8/5/2016

Dedication and my most sincere appreciation

- To the men and women haunted by the need of a father … those who spend their whole lives looking in every man for the father they miss … and are not even aware of it.
- To the father inside every man.
- To the women who have paid a high price for love just because the first man intended to love and protect them, their father, was never there for them.
- To the men who embrace their fatherhood with commitment, pride, and joy and are eager to learn how to be better fathers.
- To women who can still learn to make the best partner choice: the best father for their children.
- To the women who deserve the help of a good father for their children, and to those who have multiplied their bravery to raise children by themselves.

CONTENTS

INTRODUCTION

Fatherhood is, by nature, the basis of every relationship with males in a person's life. For boys, a father is the hero through whom they learn about manhood. For girls, a father is the model of man they are going to look up to when they choose a husband.

For over a decade, I have being listening to all types of problems in women and men, and I could always trace them to a lack of father. Little did I know that absent fatherhood was recognized as the first social problem in the United States, from where we can trace almost every other social (and I would say) individual problems. Absent fatherhood has shaken society off its normal course.

I have met girls, women, boys and girls who enjoy loving, wise and responsible fathers. Their protection, love and unconditional support have made a world of a difference in their lives. Although I consider myself a successful survivor, there is always a big possibility that my life would have been much better and easier if my father had been different.

When I was born, my father worked and lived out of town. I've been told that he saw me for the first time when I was three months old. He would visit my mother and me intermittently, without advanced notice, for birthdays, Christmas, or long weekends in the summer. The first two days of any visit were a honeymoon, but he always ended up fighting with my mom and resorting to verbal and emotional violence.

When he wasn't there, he sent us nice gifts. He provided for us financially, so my mom stayed home, waiting by the phone in case he called. Except for school, I stayed home, too, just in case. Dad didn't like it when he called and no one picked up.

My father finally came to live with Mom and me when I was twelve, and that was when my personal hell really started. Dad was more violent and abusive than ever. He constantly fought with Mom and me. He wasn't working when he came to live with us, and he never did again for reasons too complex to explain here. My mother had to get a job, and I got one when I was fourteen. I had already finished high school by then, and I helped pay my way through college, which was one of the best things I ever did for myself.

I left home and sought professional help to deal with the effects my father's abuse had on me. I became healthy enough to look after myself. I worked and studied, and I made my own life. I graduated with a bachelor's degree when I was eighteen.

Fortunately, I didn't end up a statistic, as is the case with so many other kids from fatherless families, who end up living in poverty or resorting to crime. But I do remain a part of a larger group that isn't so easily measured. There are no statistics for the overwhelming number of women and men who commit crimes against themselves: keeping themselves in constant emotional pain, choosing bad partners, living in fear and denial, struggling financially, and giving in to self-fulfilling prophecies as a result of not having good father figures.

Even those who are intellectually gifted can find themselves wandering down paths that are not in their best interests. Intelligence runs parallel to emotion. No matter how smart you are, you can still betray yourself psychologically.

However, even if you do, and even if you've been in circumstances like mine, you survive. You become an adult, and you learn to hold yourself responsible for your life. You deal with your inheritance, learn from the burden, and make decisions for yourself. And in time, you learn the importance of moving forward.

But do we ever really release the ghosts?

No. Never.

Look at what's been going on in your life lately. Does that lack of a positive father figure in your youth still haunt you today? If it does, you're not alone—and there's nothing wrong with you. It's a trait that's been imprinted on you since birth. Those of us whose fathers were absent suffer physically or emotionally from what I call "the fatherless effect" all our lives. It doesn't make us bad people. It just means we need to be careful.

The human mind is interesting, but it can also be stupid. It tends to repeat behavior and relationship patterns just because they are familiar. Even though we know that new behaviors and new ways to relate to the people around us can be healthy and even rewarding, the mind feels threatened by the unknown and makes us avoid new interactions. We get scared. Better the devil you know than the devil you don't, as the old saying goes. So we retreat to our old ways. Although they've proven to be intimidating and destructive, they're more comfortable than positive change.

And therein lies the vicious cycle. Fatherless children don't want to create fatherless families, so they become obsessed with guiding their children's destinies so that those children do not go through anything like they did. But because they never had good role models and were never taught how to make good decisions, they make bad choices that ultimately lead them back to square one.

A woman marries the wrong man, thinking he will somehow replace the father she never had. Soon her children are fatherless. Maybe her husband doesn't physically leave her, but there are a multitude of ways he can abandon a family. Sometimes, even when Daddy is home, he's not there. He's not giving his children the love they deserve. And those kids are desperate to get Daddy's attention in any way they can—even if it makes them part of the criminal statistics.

However, not all fatherless children commit crimes. In fact, I would dare say that the majority of fatherless children go in the other direction. Desperate for Daddy's approval, the children do everything they can to fulfill his expectations: good behavior, top grades at school, never stepping out of line … and still they never get what they desire. The approval, the love, and the protection never come. These children never find the healthy role models they need. They, too, are on their own.

Sometimes, the only hope we have is that our children will put an end to the curse. Thankfully, I can see that my children are headed down this path. My daughter picked the right father for her children, which is the best thing a woman can do.

Once married, women have to share the responsibilities of parenthood and give their children the time and love they need. My son, no doubt about it, will become a thoughtful, reliable father. I see in him the distinctive traits that all women should look for in their men: He is committed to behaving and, most importantly, *feeling* like a father. Men must take charge of fatherhood with all its rewards and responsibilities. They must train themselves and make themselves savvy about the matter.

Thanks to my children, I have hope; I believe that the majority of families can be saved. The statistics say that an alarming number of absent fathers, who are supposed to be there for their children, do not fulfill their roles in any way. But those numbers, those fathers, do not reflect the majority of the population. If we address these problems now, we can prevent them from getting worse in the future.

Chapter 1

WE DO LIVE IN A FATHERLESS SOCIETY

According to *The Father Factor*, publication of the National Fatherhood Initiative:

- Absentee fathers cost our nation billions of dollars a year. They negatively affect the health of children and mothers, and their children are more likely to become criminals. Even after controlling for income, youths in father-absent households had significantly higher odds of incarceration than those in mother-father families. Youths who never had a father in the household experienced the highest odds.

- A 2002 Department of Justice survey of seven thousand inmates revealed that thirty-nine percent of jail inmates lived in mother-only households. Approximately forty-six percent of jail inmates in 2002 had a previously incarcerated family member. One-fifth experienced a father in prison or jail.

- A study of 109 juvenile offenders indicated that family structure significantly predicts delinquency.

- A study of low-income minority adolescents aged ten to fourteen years found that higher social encounters and frequent communication with nonresident biological fathers decreased adolescent delinquency.

Yet while our society tackles the very serious issues of recession, health care, and war, the massive problem of fatherless children is overlooked.

The family is the basis of American society, and any negative trends in individual families are going to have a larger impact on society as a whole. Currently, our way of life is slowly eroding due to the increasing absence of the nuclear family and due to men's increasing tendencies to view their children solely as the mothers' problems.

How Many?

Twenty-five million as a rounded figure; 24.7 million according to the National Marriage Project. That's how many children are fatherless in the United States. Our entire population is 300 million, so one-twelfth of us who have grown up without good male role models in our lives. And those are only the reported cases. Just think of all the fatherless children who've never said anything. *The Father Factor* states it like this:

- Whether they're counted officially or not, children living in homes without their fathers are more likely to suffer from low birth weights, are less likely to be breastfed, are more likely to become criminals, and are less likely to achieve academically. These factors can lead to the final statistic: they're more likely to end up poorer than their fathers were. Infant mortality rates are 1.8 times higher for infants of unmarried mothers than for married mothers.

- High-quality interaction by any type of father predicts better infant health.

And the children aren't the only ones affected: Moms who struggle to raise children on their own are more likely to smoke, less likely to seek prenatal medical care, and more likely to suffer from postpartum depression.

Absent fatherhood has a deal to do with poverty. The NFI information summarizes it well:

> - Children in father-absent homes are almost four times more likely to be poor. In 2011, 12 percent of children in married-couple families were living in poverty, compared to 44 percent of children in mother-only families.
> - In 2008, American poverty rates were 13.2 percent for the whole population and 19 percent for children, compared to 28.7 percent for female-headed households.

What about emotional and behavioral problems?

- Data from three waves of the Fragile Families Study (N=2,111) was used to examine the prevalence and effects of mothers' relationship changes between birth and age three on their children's well being. Children born to single mothers show higher levels of aggressive behavior than children born to married mothers. Living in a single-mother household is equivalent to experiencing 5.25 partnership transitions.

- A sample of 4,027 resident fathers and children from the Fragile Families and Child Well-Being Survey was used to investigate the effects of a biological father's multipartner fertility (having at least one child with more than one mother) on adolescent health. Resident fathers engaging in multipartner fertility were older, more likely to be white, and had lower education levels and income compared to fathers with one partner. Results indicated children's externalizing behaviors were negatively affected directly and indirectly when their biological father had children with multiple partners.

- Being raised by a single mother raises the risk of teen pregnancy, marrying with less than a high school degree, and forming a marriage where both partners have less than a high school degree.

- Separation or frequent changes increase a woman's risk of early menarche, sexual activity, and pregnancy. Women whose parents separated between birth and six years old experienced twice the risk of early menstruation, more than four times the risk of early sexual intercourse, and two and a half times higher risk of early pregnancy when compared to women in intact families. The longer a woman lived with both parents, the lower her risk of early reproductive development. Women who experienced three or more changes in her family environment exhibited similar risks but were five times more likely to have an early pregnancy.

Does absent fatherhood relate to child abuse?

We quote the NFI again:

- A study using data from the Fragile Families and Child Wellbeing Study revealed that in many cases, the absence of a biological father contributes to increased risk of child maltreatment. The results suggest that Child Protective Services (CPS) agencies have some justification in viewing the presence of a social father as increasing children's risk of abuse and neglect. It is believed that in families with a nonbiological (social) father figure, there is a higher risk of abuse and neglect to children, despite the social father living in the household or only dating the mother.
- In a study examining father-related factors predicting maternal physical child abuse risk, researchers conducted interviews with mothers of three-year-old children. The results revealed that mothers who were married to fathers were at lower risk for maternal physical child abuse. Moreover, it was found that higher educational attainment and positive father involvement with their children were significant predictors of lower maternal physical child abuse risk.

Drug and Alcohol Abuse

- Even after controlling for community context, there is significantly more drug use among children who do not live with both their mother and father.
- In a study of 6,500 children from the ADDHEALTH database, father closeness was negatively correlated with the number of a child's friends who smoke, drink, and smoke marijuana. Closeness was also correlated with a child's use of alcohol, cigarettes, and hard drugs and was connected to family structure. Intact families ranked higher on father closeness than single-parent families.

Education

- Father involvement in schools is associated with a higher likelihood of a student getting mostly As. This was true for fathers in biological parent families, for stepfathers, and for fathers heading single-parent families.
- A study assessing 4,109 two-parent families examined the effects of early maternal and paternal depression on child expressive language at age twenty-four months and the role that parent-to-child reading may play in child's language development. The results revealed that, for mothers and fathers, depressive symptoms were negatively associated with parent-to-child reading. Only for fathers, however, was earlier depression associated with later reading to child and related child expressive vocabulary

development. The less the fathers read to their infants, the worse their toddler scored on a standard measure of expressive vocabulary at age two. Parents' depression has more impact on how often fathers read to their child compared to mothers, which in turn influences the child's language development.

All of these statistics, though, are just a small drop in the bucket. Children who grow up without a father often experience emotional problems that can't be calculated or compared to children growing up in a traditional family. The psychological effects of abandonment almost always follow these children into adulthood and can last a lifetime. For example, women who were raised without fathers tend to search their entire lives for replacements, jumping from one abusive relationship to another, and boys will model their behaviors on any father figures they can find—from criminals to strangers to people they see on TV. As you can imagine, as they grow into men, their concepts of what it means to be a man can be quite skewed.

The resentment such kids feel toward not just their fathers but their mothers and the world in general is profound, and it takes a terrible toll on their abilities to form solid and stable homes for their own children.

Millions of men in our society feel perfectly justified in fathering children they don't intend to support, and millions of women feel powerless to do anything about it. The causes behind this predicament are complicated, and the fix for our fatherless nation will not be easy. It will take a conscious decision by men and their families to foster, encourage, and demand different and better behaviors. Without concerted efforts from people on all sides of the issue, the problem is likely to only get worse.

A Common Misconception

Discussions of absentee fathers commonly focus on those who are physically absent from the home, but I will not make that mistake in this book. Yes, we will look at fathers who live apart from their children and the mothers of their children, but we will also examine the phenomenon of absentee fathers who still live in the family home. Though this might seem contradictory, it is more common than we would like to believe. Men don't have to be gone to be absent; they can still be there, providing all the material things they think their children need, though some of them don't even provide financially.

Men like this are trying to do the right thing, but they don't understand that just being in the home is not enough. Physical presence alone does not give their children the support and encouragement they need. Unfortunately, some fathers are simply too lazy or callous to get more involved. The children of such fathers suffer many of the same social and psychological consequences as their counterparts in single-parent homes.

The Reward for Change

Some men view fatherhood as a burden, something that will cost them both time and money. To them, children are anchors that keep them from living independent lives. Of course, those are lies—fatherhood is an incredibly rewarding and enriching endeavor. It contributes not only to healthier families but to healthier neighborhoods, healthier cultures, and a healthier society.

And when fathers take active, concerned roles in their families' lives, moms win too. Having a partner to help raise children is invaluable. Many women have been taught that they don't need men to raise their children, and while some single women can produce healthy, productive children, there is no substitute for the balance and strength of a couple working together. There is an old saying: "It takes a village to raise a child." That is so true! Figure out how hard it is for only one person to raise a child!

Shared parenting reduces stress on the mother and allows her to explore life and career options, and it provides a male role model for the children—who are the biggest winners of all in this equation. I cannot stress enough how important it is for children to have present, involved dads who care about them and who can provide positive examples of male behavior. Even small moments, like seeing their father at a school event or watching Mom and Dad dance together, can have such a positive impact on the way children rate the importance of family.

Some—myself included—will say that fatherhood is a reward unto itself. Men can gain so much from accepting and fulfilling their parenting responsibilities: increased self-worth and self-esteem, a sense of accomplishment, pride in themselves and their children—the list goes on and on.

Unfortunately, men are not always told that fatherhood can be such a wonderful experience, especially if they were raised without fathers themselves. As a society, we must change the way we raise our boys to encourage better fathering and to bring them, when they become men, into the parenting fold.

However, this cannot be accomplished through degradation or threats. Instead, we must show men that fatherhood is a rewarding, positive experience no matter how hard it might be. They must see fatherhood as a service they can provide their children, their wives, their communities, and even themselves. They must understand the vital role they play in our culture.

Chapter 2

CAUSES YOU WOULDN'T LIKE TO ADMIT

Why does our society push men away from fatherhood? How has it become acceptable for so many men to leave women alone to raise their children? The causes behind the phenomenon are many, but at the very core is the way men's and women's roles have shifted over the years. Many of these changes have been positive, but the fallout has sometimes been negative—a mixed bag that has both helped and hurt us.

The transformation didn't happen overnight. It's been a progressive change dating back to the early days of our nation, when women had few rights. Men the world over have a long track record of marginalizing and subjugating women, and our country was no different. You can see the effects of this behavior in many of today's societal and religious traditions, such as the corporate "glass ceiling" or the refusal of many Christian sects to allow women to become members of the clergy. In addition, equal pay and harassment-free workplaces are still elusive goals for many women.

However, the women's-rights movement has made some remarkable advancements:

- The right to vote, ratified in the Nineteenth Amendment of August 18, 1920
- Acknowledgement of the right to birth control in 1936
- Laws requiring fair hiring practices, paid maternity leave, and the right to affordable child care in 1961
- The Equal Pay Act, approved in 1963
- Title VII of the Civil Rights Act of 1964, barring discrimination in employment on basis of race and sex
- Sexual harassment acknowledged as discrimination of gender under Title II of the 1964 Civil Rights Act
- The 1967 executive order barring discrimination by gender, giving the same educational and employment opportunities that white males enjoy, and making clear that women cannot be paid less
- Laws against discrimination in the educational system, in Title IX of the 1972 Education Act
- The 1974 Equal Credit Opportunity Act prohibiting discrimination on the basis of gender
- 1976 law declaring it illegal to rape a wife
- Pregnancy Discrimination Act of 1978 stating that women cannot be fired or denied a promotion due to pregnancy
- The 1994 Violence Against Women Act
- 2009 Lily Redbetter Fair Pay Restoration Act, providing the right to sue
- The 2013 Revitalization of the 1994 Violence Against Women Act

While fighting for equal treatment in the United States, women as a group in the last century have asserted themselves as never before. With an attitude that they can do anything their husbands or male counterparts can do, women have become scientists, doctors, engineers, and pilots, just to name a few of their accomplishments.

But while this can-do attitude has been beneficial for some women, where has it left those whose situations are more complicated? Women who are married to emotionally absent husbands might struggle to do it all—raise a family, pursue a career, and prove themselves equal counterparts to men—making life very easy for their children's fathers while they carry the whole burden of their households.

And what about single mothers who've been left to raise children on their own due to bad experiences with their male partners? How are they to attain the same level of success?

Both situations are fraught with negative consequences for any children involved, leaving them with less attention and support than they need and deserve.

Still, many in the women's-rights movement want women to think that independence means never needing help. Even when your child's father tells you that caring for a baby is woman's work and not his job, even when the estranged father of your children has no interest in the lives of his offspring, you are not only supposed to make it on your own but to excel, to *rise above* somehow and show that you can do it all.

Understandably, such expectations can cause some pretty big resentments between women and men, and so in the fervor to overthrow chauvinist attitudes, we've developed a kind of *us* versus *them* attitude. It started as a rift, a natural consequence of conflict in the struggle for equal treatment, and unfortunately some people took it too far. Eventually, we found ourselves asking, "Men? Who needs 'em?"

Many women who have had bad experiences with the fathers of their children, especially those who have been abandoned, have adopted the attitude, as a defense mechanism, that men aren't really needed in the home. Even though deep down they miss the support their male partners could provide and are hurt by the rejection, they rationalize the situation to protect themselves from further pain. "I can do without him," they say to themselves and everyone else in an effort to cope with the absence and keep on living. Eventually, they start believing the lie.

Women, of course, will not die without men in their lives. But what toll does this independence have on their children? Are they really better off without a father figure? When the father is a threat to life, safety, or well-being, a single-parent home is optimal for a child. In a nurturing relationship in which the father takes on his part of responsibility, the best option for children and Mom is a two-parent family.

Some psychological schools of thought call the social need for a partner *codependence.* Others posit that those who feel this need suffer from low self-esteem. Still others tell women that they don't really *need* men, they just *want* men, as though having a father in the home is a luxury that shouldn't be expected. It should be expected, looked for, and deserved by Mom and the kids.

The Lesson

Parenthood is a permanent partnership. It is teamwork. Stop perceiving parenthood as division of labor under which the mother is in charge of the children. It takes two to create a baby; it also takes two to form its character and shape its future. Because men have not been taught that fatherhood is a worthy and rewarding endeavor, and because women have been pressured to "do it all" without the help of men, we find ourselves unable to work together on one of the most important collaborations there is: parenthood. We must work together to get past this crossroads and become appropriate role models for our children, to give them a fighting chance in this world.

Chapter 3

SUPERMOM: PHYSICAL AND EMOTIONAL EXHAUSTION

Let's face it: Families need men. Children need fathers. And while women are incredibly competent and capable of doing things on their own, that does not mean that it is convenient for them to lead a stressful life that leaves them exhausted at the end of the day.

Women's-rights activists have gone too far in marginalizing the roles of men in today's families. Equal rights, equal work, and equal salaries are rights that all women deserve, but many women are trying to do everything at once. We're each trying to be Supermom, and it just isn't working, and women and families are hurting because of this.

The Supermom lifestyle developed as women struggled for equality in the workplace and men gave up their responsibilities. While women fought for jobs never before held by people of their gender, they continued having children, and thus was born the work-life balancing act that so many of us contend with today.

In reality, however, there is rarely any balance when a woman tries to develop both career and family, especially when she does it on her own. Without help from a significant other, a woman is forced to work long hours and then dedicate any remaining time in the day to her children. This mad scramble can leave children without the valuable parenting time they deserve. It can even deprive their mothers of energy, mental health, and a balanced, happy life.

There are, of course, exceptions to the ideal two-parent home—scenarios in which women must make it work by themselves. This includes those who have no choice but to act as both Mom and Dad because there is nobody around to help them, and those who have help but believe their lives should reflect what they see in women's magazines—that they should be thin, beautiful career women who dote on their children while getting master's degrees and acting as the family's gourmet chef. Others have husbands who refuse to help them.

Another rarer class of women are those with husbands who are willing to help but don't know how. Men respond to direct communication. A woman should never expect her partner to guess how, when, or where she will need to be helped, but unfortunately, many of us do that. We expect our men to anticipate our every need—or the needs of our family—even when we give no sign of what we lack.

The most obvious solution to this particular problem is to tell our partners when we need help. And we must be specific. Give them tasks and show them how to do things they haven't done before, and help them learn to be great parents. Men are perfectly capable of supporting you in your role as mother. Sometimes all you have to do is let them.

I know, unfortunately, that this is not the case for many women. Many work hard to support their children with little or no help. For them, the only alternative is to become a Supermom because they are fighting two battles: their real-life present situation and the generational baggage they learned from their mothers and preceding family.

These Supermoms fall into different classifications, but they share similar traits. There are different ways women end up being forced to become Supermom.

#1 Supermom: The Womanizer's Wife

There is a Supermom who has been a professional woman since she was in her early twenties. She fell in love with a tall, handsome man with movie-star looks who swept her off her feet. He was romantic, good, helping, thoughtful, and she thought he was perfect (her first mistake).

Unfortunately, he turned out to be the perfect wolf in sheep's clothing. But Supermom didn't realize it, and she married him after a month-long courtship (her second mistake).

Her husband turned out to be emotionally manipulative and psychologically abusive, but he did not hit her as he had other women, and so she stayed with him. He also cheated, but she had been raised to believe that all men were expected to be unfaithful, that it was just a part of marriage (a personal shortcoming due to socialization and low self-esteem). She realized that he was unreliable, irresponsible, and not really committed to the idea of a two-way relationship, but she did not think that she had a choice. This Supermom had been raised by an abusive father and a submissive mother and could not imagine a different type of marriage. Looking the other way was part of her job as the wife.

Of course, this Supermom and her husband fought frequently, after which he always promised her things in return for forgiveness (signs of dysfunctional interaction). During one reconciliation, he promised her that he was ready to become a father. She wanted a baby, and she got pregnant. But nothing had changed in her husband's underlying character, and he did not change his inexcusable behavior. He just became more discreet in his cheating.

Now, long before she was a Supermom, this young lady was a superwoman. Since the beginning of her marriage, she had a full-time job and worked overtime twice a week, cooked dinner five days a week (and three meals a day on weekends), did laundry and other chores, cleaned the house, ran errands, and did all the grocery shopping. She even laid out her husband's clothes every night for the next day. On top of all of that, when she gave birth to a girl, she was also completely in charge of the child. Dad played with the baby only when he felt like it.

He did, however, find time to cheat on her once again, and this time was the last straw. Going up against her husband's will, Supermom asked for divorce. He threatened her, of course, but she persisted. In the settlement, she got a small amount of money to buy a house and cover moving expenses. The Supermom who had carried her family was now physically alone. Dad paid almost nothing in child support, and she carried almost all the burden herself. He would show up to see his daughter when he had nothing else to do (and so he said every time).

To make ends meet, Supermom got a temporary, part-time, home-based job. On Saturdays, she handled the laundry, cleaning, and grocery shopping, all with her daughter in tow. On Sundays, she usually found a little time to rest and actually enjoy being a mother. Whenever she could throughout the week, she fit in every detail related to raising a child: managing the financial burden, going to the pediatrician, dealing with emergencies, attending parents' meetings, getting props for special events at school, hosting play dates and birthday parties, and answering every question her daughter asked.

She wanted to be energetic, to make her daughter feel that her mother was there for her. She built a supportive relationship … but at what cost? Was she successful, anyway, in sparing her child the consequences? No!

Despite her best intentions and all her love, her child suffered some consequences. First, since Mom and Dad (however he behaves) are the role models, the child may conclude that these dynamics are normal and expected. In her adulthood, she may repeat them (worst-case scenario) or create exactly the opposite situation. Unfortunately, chances are she will repeat this type of relationship.

Second, but not less important, the child will unconsciously create a need for the supportive, loving, responsible father she didn't have, with all the emotional shortcomings this situation brings.

Solutions?

1- If you are not in this situation yet, please make the right choice of partner. I will be stressing repeatedly the importance of choosing the right life partner. Please, choose the right partner consciously and then fall in love with him. It doesn't work the other way around, even if TV and movies tell you otherwise.

2- If you are already in this situation, seek professional help. Why? Because if you made such a selection, you will go on being manipulated enough to keep on believing that it's your only choice. You need to gain insight into what you are doing to yourself and what you are doing to your children.

3- If, after you do #2, the man is open to being trained and to modifying his behavior, decide whether you are going to give him a chance or not. If you end up breaking up or if his behavior persists, help your child to avoid repeating your pattern.

4- If you feel helpless, if you are in denial, or if you think that you cannot have a healthy environment for you and your child, please seek professional counseling.

#2 Supermom: The Nice (but Not So Perfect) Husband's Wife

There is another Supermom whose circumstances are quite different. She met this guy and admired his gentle manners and strong family values. He was and is hard working at his job or profession. They got married after a decent period of dating, but she never found out nor even asked herself if he was able to share household duties or take care of children.

He is a good husband who treats her nicely, does not cheat, and loves her and their children unconditionally. We'd all say that she pretty much has it made, right?

Unfortunately, looks can be deceiving, and while a decent husband is definitely someone to treasure, it does not necessarily mean that he is a good partner when it comes to running a household. The worst of it is that this guy's wife most likely feels privileged for having this type of husband, and she either doesn't want to "rock the boat" by asking him for help at home, or she really believes she should be the one to shoulder all the household burdens. By the way, if you think that talking to your husband can "rock the boat," "the boat" is already sunk.

This man is the kind who doesn't help with the daily work it takes to keep a family going. He was raised to be lazy about housework; his father told him that his only job was to provide financially for his family and that household chores were meant for his wife, even if she had a full-time job. His mother did everything for him: cooking, cleaning, laundry, and all the household chores and never trained him to help.

Sure enough, he unconsciously (or maybe very consciously) chose a wife or partner who was very similar to his mother. Most nights, this husband comes home from work, takes a shower, grabs his remote control, and watches TV from the comfort of his easy chair. He never cooks, does laundry, cleans, does household chores, or helps with the children.

To his credit, this husband loves to play with the children, but whenever they have a problem—tough homework, a fight with a friend, a fight among themselves—he is not there to help them. That's Mommy's job. No one at the children's school knows him at all because he never drops them off or attends school events; most of the time he finds excuses not to attend. Most likely he just has no idea how to deal with this type of situation.

To make up for this, Supermom does everything for everybody. Sometimes she thinks it's unfair, but other times she merely accepts it as the way things are. Sometimes she feels like a heroine and falls into the trap of telling herself, "Oh, I'm so great and capable!" However, at the end of the day, when her husband wants her attention, she has none left—and he wonders why. He is aloof and totally unaware of what is going on.

What are the consequences? At first, Dad feels like a king because he is not held responsible for anything. This is why the children rely on Supermom for everything. She controls expressions of love and information because children tend to stick to the person who pays the most attention, solves their problems, and is always there for them.

Dad feels dismissed and left out and is the last one in the family to find out what is happening around him, if he ever finds out. Of course, he has no idea how to deal with this. He feels upset and blames Mom. Chances are that he cannot accept that he has been an absentee father by his own behavior; he is sure that he is on the right track and that everybody else is wrong.

Family life becomes tough. Worst of all, the message delivered to the children is that Mom and Dad are in disagreement but that Mom is the solving, loving parent. You don't want to see the kind of family these children will have when it is their turn to have families.

Solutions?

1- If you are married to a good, loving man, observe how he was raised and be ready to reeducate him. Start the training before you tie the knot. If you think his upbringing was good, start training yourself. Be brave enough to accept that you want a balanced family life and not an exhausting one.

2- Avoid bitter criticism toward a behavior that was there from the beginning. Entice your husband toward cooperation, and reward his adjustment to new behaviors.

3- Remember that the behaviors people grow up with are imprinted and do not change overnight. When you think that they may have changed, they may appear again. Be patient if the man is, overall, worth it.

4- Be honest and straightforward. First, let him know you need his help. Second, reward him for becoming more involved with his children. That will empower him emotionally, and he will feel proud of being knowledgeable about his children's life and everything happening in the house.

5- Keep this in mind. You may think that he likes his passive role. In the long run, that's wrong. Men have a great necessity to feel needed … and this works to your and your children's best interests.

#3 Supermom: The Control Freak (Nobody Does It Better Than Her)

Blinded by a combination of hubris and a need to control others, another species of Supermom believes that nobody does anything as well as she does. Her motto is, "If I want things to be done the right way, I have to do them myself." She demands perfection and she thinks she does everything so perfectly that she prefers her husband to not even try to help out around the house. He sees her struggling with chores, putting in a lot of time and energy, and he wants to help. He can cook and be somewhat handy around the house, and he loves to be involved with the children. He'll even change their diapers and feed them.

When the husband is allowed to share responsibilities, he is put down with severe criticism because "he doesn't know how to do it" or because "he did it wrong." Indeed, #3 Supermom offers no gratitude and no positive reinforcement. She can even make humiliating remarks and never says "thank you."

By the way, this is the type of woman who wouldn't hire a cleaning lady because nobody cleans as well as she does, but she then complains about feeling so exhausted at the end of the week. If she hires the cleaning lady, she cleans before the cleaning lady comes in. She is so perfect that nothing anyone else does will satisfy her.

She takes pride in telling everybody that the husband and the children do nothing and boasts about being a multitasking woman and that they cannot do without her. Sometimes she is tempted to play the victim role for no reason, but of course she thinks that she has every reason on her side.

As if this behavior were not damaging enough, this Supermom prefers to exhaust herself or to die because she has a hard time asking for and accepting help. She nonetheless blames everybody for not helping her.

Where does that Supermom come from? Either from an extremely competitive family or from one in which the parents demanded perfection and made their love conditional on her living up to their expectations.

Maybe, during her childhood, significant others put her down all the time, or she experienced strong and deep feelings of insecurity and didn't trust others. Perhaps she had an extreme need for recognition or was raised with the concept that it is wrong to ask for help because it shows weakness. Or maybe hers was a very sloppy family who made her feel embarrassed in front of her peers—and she chose exactly the opposite behavior for herself.

Consequences?

1- If Dad does not have enough self-esteem, he may feel useless and undermined. That causes resentfulness that will damage the marital relationship and the children.

2- The children might at first think that Mom has a real reason for not allowing Dad to do anything. But children are extremely perceptive and sooner or later will notice that Supermom's attitude is to blame. They will be resentful toward Mom and more loving to Dad. This may create an imbalance that is not good for the family, the children, or their relationship with their father.

3- Man is deprived of his father role.

Solutions?

1- Mom has to train herself to skip her roles as savior, rescuer, victim, and Mrs. Perfect. She also has to deal with her control issues.

2- She has to replace the word *perfect* with *very good* and *excellent*. She has to stop striving for perfection because that puts an enormous burden upon her and her family. Besides, *perfection* brings so much stress that she can put her physical health in jeopardy.

3- Mom has to develop the patience to allow Dad to help her and establish his own relationships with the children, for the sake of everybody's mental health.

4- And, please, Mom, wouldn't you like to be recognized for who you are and not for what you do? Wouldn't you like to be unconditionally loved for the person you are instead of conditionally loved for whatever perfect things you do for others?

5- Learn to *ask for help* and accept it. Learn this. The best man on Earth has to specifically be *asked* for help. Men are not good at second-guessing.

Necessary Change

When we look at these Supermoms, we see reflections of the larger issues that have produced so many fatherless families in America. The shifting roles of men and women in our society have empowered many women, but they have also led some to believe that they must carry the world on their own. At the same time, these shifts have caused many men to believe that they are no longer responsible for raising their families.

Unfortunately, many women have allowed these perceptions to fester, and that is in part what created the Supermom phenomenon. But is there any way that we can throw off this role if we learn to make better choices for ourselves and our families?

In the examples above, the #1 Supermom has no choice other than to do it all alone. Her husband provides nothing but fear and disappointment, so she must depend on herself for her physical and emotional needs. To combat this, she should examine how she arrived at that point in order to avoid repeating the pattern when she looks for a new partner. If she understands how her past choices affected her life, she will make better choices in the future.

#2 Supermom and #3 Supermom still have the option of getting their husbands involved—all they have to do is put forth a little effort and include them more in the family. It's never too late to teach a man about his responsibilities or to ask for help when you need it. This will be easier for #3 Supermom, but not impossible for #2 Supermom. Training, love, reinforcement and trust can lead to more balanced lives for women who find themselves in similar situations.

Supermom … Don't Make It That Easy!

For a long time in our society, men had too much control. As self-established power figures, they granted women few rights, and naturally, women fought back against that.

In came the women's-rights movement, which helped us gain social footing and win the rights we deserved. And then we kept on fighting. And finally, the pendulum swung too far the other way. Unintentionally, the women's liberation movement has enslaved many unsuspecting women.

In earlier generations, women had full-time jobs at home, taking care of their families, their children, and their households.

Traditionally, the man of the house knew that he was meant to be the provider—financially. Much of the time, he didn't think he had to help much more than that. However, he indisputably honored his responsibility as provider and protector. Some women did not have the unbearable stress of asking themselves whether their husbands and the fathers of their children were going to abandon them financially.

That was a very different lifestyle from what we are used to today, when wives hold multiple jobs outside the home and are still expected to care for their children and their households—and please their men in any way possible.

Much of the time, they do so quite willingly, eager to show that they can do it all, that they are just as capable of running their families as their men are. However, in their zeal, women have forgotten that equality doesn't mean this sort of imbalance. We have fought for our rights and gained our independence, and that has benefited society on the whole a great deal. But it's also spread us thin. And what does that do for our families and children?

American families these days are out of balance, and I believe that this is due in large part to the fact that we have taken responsibility from men, making life too convenient and easy for them. As women have accepted and gained more and more responsibility, men have stepped back from it and even relinquished their authority. In many ways, men react with laziness, indifference, and anger.

It seems that at some time in our history, women learned to operate without the help of men because men left because of war, hunting, and migration, leaving the families absent a father figure. In other instances, men have been unreliable. We women believed we could do it all on our own, but that is unfair for us. Some women do not even claim for child support when they are left alone with their children. Others relinquish their children's rights for child support. All that burden—financial physical and emotional—is unrealistic. It is just another example of the decisions we make as women every day, decisions that create self-fulfilling prophecies. And it's time that we stopped that.

Instead of dismissing men as unreliable or uninterested in raising their children, women should expect and demand their men be involved in growing and supporting their families. Women must make men understand that they have responsibilities and that women cannot and should not do everything by themselves. Mothers of male children must raise them with a clear understanding of the need to become a responsible father and a household helper.

Women need to hand over half the parenting responsibilities to their men and expect them to get involved with their children at higher levels, especially if the women are working full time. Even if a man is the main financial provider, the woman must make an effort to get him involved in parenting and to act as a role model. It is time to make men feel the significance of fatherhood and the need that their families have for them.

I am not putting the blame for absentee or abusive fathers on women—not at all. I am saying that we must understand our own roles in these situations and do what we can to remedy them. Women have great influence in their families; in most households, mothers are the most influential, especially when it comes to educating their children. And what are we teaching them? That women are responsible for nearly all household duties and that it's okay if fathers are lazy or disinterested. By doing this, we're setting ourselves up for conflict with our future children-in-law, because when our sons and daughters marry, what sorts of traditions are they going to carry over into their own homes?

Over time, we've helped develop dysfunctional, unbalanced families, and that has affected society at large. The good news is that we can change it. Let us start it at home, raising sons the right way for the best future of fatherhood.

The Lesson

The women's-rights movement, for all the good things it has done, has had negative consequences as well. Today, women are more overwhelmed than ever before. Being encouraged to do it all by yourself is more like slavery than liberation, and out of that has come a generation of wives and mothers who feel trapped in their roles rather than enjoying them. To overcome this situation and set things right, we must look at ourselves and understand how the choices we've made have put us into the situations we're in today.

We must also hold our men accountable for their responsibilities as fathers and husbands. If we do, we might just be surprised by how willing they are to fill these roles.

Chapter 4

ABSENTEE FATHERS OF ALL STRIPES

These days, we encourage our daughters to be anyone they want and to do anything they desire—and they can. That's a wonderful accomplishment for a society that wouldn't allow women to vote less than a century ago.

But what about our sons? Women have educated themselves and have made contributions in such areas as science, medicine, law, and engineering, but as a society, we still lag in educating men about their familial roles.

With any shift in society, there is a ripple effect. As women have been encouraged to go out into the field, build careers, and contribute to our workforce, we have neglected how this has affected the men in our lives. With women out at work all day, men are needed at home more than ever. Nature doesn't like a vacuum, and when one parent is out of the home, the other needs to fill that void. But we haven't adapted the way we educate our sons to reflect that need. Consistently, generation after generation, we have accepted and fostered the concept of father as provider and strong authority figure. We have allowed our men—and in some cases enticed them—to remain aloof from what family really is. Men, at first, resented this attitude, but in time they just went with it because they felt comfortable being free of responsibilities, and women let men get away with it because they did not want to fight. We deride men for their lack of fatherly behavior, but they are not solely to blame. Mothers and other significant women have fostered it as well.

The upbringing of a baby boy is very particular. Upon his birth, everybody in the family, male and female, celebrates what he represents: the continuation of the family name. As he grows, they all do their best to make sure he copies all the traditional male behaviors, both positive and negative. In this way, most of the time, we raise future fathers who are ill-prepared for what their families and their society will need. Hence, we live in an era when more and more families are without fathers.

Our society now comprises millions of families without an effective paternal presence. We complain about how frequently fathers abandon their children, but we do not raise boys to become responsible fathers. Instead, we make men feel incompetent and unnecessary when it comes to their children. We alienate them from the process of childrearing, and the consequences are dire.

And what, then, becomes of their children? Boys and girls who grow up without fathers turn into men and women who search for father-figure substitutes and end up in abusive relationships or with mentors who don't have their best interests in mind.

Sometimes, we even encourage this; we've convinced ourselves that a boy can find a father figure in any good man, even if the man is not his biological father. But we're wrong. Children need their fathers, and women need good husbands who are willing to be good fathers. Our society is based on the family unit, and it is falling apart. It's an understatement to say that the fallout is terrible.

When most people think of a fatherless family, they imagine a woman alone with her kids, trying to raise them by herself. And that's exactly what many fatherless families look like. However, they come in many forms.

The Man Who Divorces His Wife—and His Children

Some men consider divorce a complete severance. In ending their marriages to their wives, they also abandon all emotional and financial responsibility for their children—and then believe that they have the right to create new lives without their kids. They seem to forget that their children have the same financial needs that they had when their parents were married and that their children need food on their tables and clothes on their backs.

In such situations, children are hurt because they can't understand that they are not to blame. Children tend to blame themselves as if they were factors in the divorce even when they were not. They have a hard time reconciling their feelings of guilt, anger, and shame. What's more, they don't understand why their fathers chose to sever all ties with them, and the fathers are not around to tell their side of the story. So the children miss out not just on the time they'd spend with their fathers but also on the trust that could be built through such interactions.

These children of divorce tend to grow up conflicted: they look for partners, but they also think that all marriages are doomed to fail. Usually, they keep themselves closed off emotionally to protect themselves against the pain of failed relationships. When they do manage to extend themselves far enough to find partners and marry, they either repeat the process and divorce or overcompensate in the opposite direction, doing everything they can to keep even dysfunctional relationships afloat.

Some girls who grow up in homes affected by divorce later look for older men as partners. In search of the guidance, protection, security, and love they did not receive from their fathers, they seek out men who will do everything for them; in the process, they negate their own thoughts, opinions, and feelings. These women aren't looking for relationships built on equally shared responsibility; they are perpetuating an already broken cycle.

Other women from divorced families go the other route and choose unreliable or abusive men who put them back into the scenario of the fatherless home. Having been abandoned by their fathers after the divorce, these women—and men who have survived the same situations—are left with emotional scars that tear at their self-esteem.

The Abusive Father

Kids of abusive fathers can grow up thinking that every father is like theirs. Usually, these kids don't find out until they are older that their fathers were anything but normal. Unfortunately, the damage to their psyches is done well before they come to such an understanding, and so they find themselves continually returning to what they know—abusive, dysfunctional relationships—even if they know it is wrong.

The good news is that some children raised by abusive fathers respond by saying, "This isn't going to happen to me," and as adults, they look for partners who are not abusive, effectively breaking the cycle. The downside? Sometimes they overdo it to the point that they delay entering meaningful relationships until later in their lives. I've seen women who waited until they were in their thirties to marry because they were overly cautious, afraid that their husbands would end up like their abusive fathers. They've denied themselves the joys of having good partners because they can't put their faith in anyone. And can you blame them? If your own parent violated your trust and love, could you expect a stranger to be a good partner?

The worst-case scenario, and the one that speaks most starkly to the subject of violation, involves a father who is sexually abusive. Fatherhood is supposed to be about love, mutual trust, respect, and role modeling, but when sexual abuse enters the picture, those tenets can become irreparably broken. There is no way a sexually abused child can come out of it and easily make the best partner selection without getting any professional help. The first significant male figure in this child's life betrayed his or her trust in a most horrible way, and the damage will be lasting and devastating. Professional help and support are often required for a sexual-abuse survivor to recover and engage in healthy relationships.

Though some might give a father who abuses his children physically or emotionally a pass because at least he is present in his children's lives, in truth he is an absentee father because he is too busy dealing with his own psychosis to effectively handle the responsibilities of raising a family. He can't be consulted in any serious matters, and he destroys the family's self-esteem across the board. The effects of an abusive father's actions are lifelong and determine the course of all future relationships for his children.

The Sole-Provider Father

Often, the sole-provider type of father is very rich. This isn't a problem in itself, but when he sees money as the only way to show affection to his children—well, therein lies the beginning of this family's dysfunction.

The sole-provider father is never home because he works most of the time. He doesn't go to his kids' school functions or sports games because that's Mom's job—she's in charge of everything having to do with the children, the family, and the home. In essence, in this situation, Mom doesn't have a husband, and the children don't have a father. What they have is a guy who gives the money and expects it to be enough.

Children usually exhibit one of two reactions to this type of upbringing. In the first, they take advantage of their father's money because that is all they know they will get from him. Their parents—their absentee dad and their Supermom—never challenge them or tell them they can't have something; as a result, they are spoiled, and they lash out when they don't get their way. They have no boundaries, and as the children grow older, they might turn to substance abuse, criminal mischief or other self-destructive behavior as a means of crying for help.

Perhaps the worst effect of the sole-provider father's lack of involvement, however, is that it leaves his children with a deep inability to develop emotional intimacy with anyone. This is not surprising, as most fathers who work too much are themselves subconsciously unable to cope with intimacy. Deprived of their father's love and attention, these children—especially the daughters, who really long for their fathers—might insist that Dad's money isn't enough and try to pressure him into giving them more emotional support by causing trouble or doing bad things.

Unfortunately, many sole-provider fathers never heed their children's cries. Too mired in their own destructive patterns, they remain in denial of their own wrongdoing. They convince themselves that because they are the family breadwinners and do not let the family want for material possessions, they are in the right, and they feel resentful that their children and wives don't seem to appreciate their efforts.

The Dead Father

When a father dies, his children feel a great number of emotions. If he was abusive, there might be relief that he is gone. His children might forgive him his transgressions, especially if he died in circumstances that were out of his control, but the aftereffects of his behavior will still be long lasting. If his death was a result of his not taking care of himself, the children might also feel anger and a sense of abandonment.

If a man who had been a very good father dies accidentally, the grieving process is somewhat different. There is anger, but mostly there is grief, and the sense of abandonment remains.

Added to this is a feeling of great injustice. His children might not understand why such a good father had to be taken away from them. Such circumstances create confusion for children of all ages.

Even if a father is absent because he has died, his children still need a father figure in their lives and often will be unwilling to accept a substitute. They might also become overprotective of their remaining family members or rebellious to authority. They'll need support from their mothers and possibly even professional help to move on, find peace, and accept new relationships in their lives.

The Father Who Abandons His Family

All too often, young men believe they have no responsibility to their offspring. They believe that the women they sleep with are responsible for preventing pregnancy, and if pregnancy occurs, it's entirely the women's fault. These men abandon their children out of selfishness and do not care or even know about the consequences.

In many instances, that is what they saw in their own homes. They cannot give out what they did not receive. Yes, there are men who were abandoned by fathers and who don't abandon their children for that very reason. However, that is the exception. On the other hand, raising a son without teaching him responsibility for his own acts can also cause that son to grow up and abandon his offspring.

The consequence of this fatherly neglect and rejection can cause emotional imbalance and delinquency in their children and can affect the way those children end up raising their own families. They choose to either learn to be good parents or to repeat their fathers' mistakes simply out of resentment.

The Truly Absent Father

While some fathers are constantly away from home because they work a lot to provide for their families, others stay away simply because they crave the independence they had when they were single. Such fathers don't provide for their families in any form or take any responsibility for the people who depend on them. They might come to the family house to fulfill everyday needs, such as eating, sleeping, and bathing, but they make their lives entirely outside the home as if they had no family at all.

That brings us to a lack of maturity in such men. They decided to commit without being ready or even aware of what they were doing. The cause? That behavior is often due to being raised as a narcissistic child who was not taught the proper self-control.

The Shell of a Father

Many fathers never learned what it means to be actively involved in their children's lives. They think that their physical presence is enough, that just being around constitutes fathering. They leave the emotional things to the children's mother, who often doesn't know how to get him more involved, and so the cycle of absenteeism and unbalanced responsibility continues.

A shell of a father really thinks that his children are his wife's responsibility at all times—or, at least, until they get disrespectful or behave badly. Then the father will intervene, asserting himself as the strong, fearful power figure who straightens everybody out. This, he believes, is the image a father must project, but as a result, the relationships he develops with his children are largely negative. They perceive him as the bad, unfair guy instead of the loving, supportive role model they need and want.

The Ignorant Father

A great number of fathers want to do the right thing for their children and partners. They are full of commitment, love, and goodwill, but they have no clue what they need to do. What are their responsibilities? What should they be doing for their wives and sons and daughters? How are they supposed to do it? What is expected from them? They don't know, and no one is telling them because we as a society have not made teaching parenting skills to men as much of a priority as developing parenting skills in women.

In most occidental cultures, girls are involved at an early age in playing with dolls and pretending they are "mommies." Most of them have toys evoking household chores, and as children, they tend to imitate Mommy, who is the direct role model. Boys are still raised for sports and rough games, but of course they are not introduced to dolls or any primitive parenting skill. So if being a mother does not come naturally to all women, fathering definitely does not come naturally unless that boy has a good role model in father figure he can imitate.

Most of the time, these good men who do not know any better as fathers grew up without the right role model. Remember that children learn by copying behavior. If a boy did not have a father who took his fatherhood seriously and instructed the child about that role, that boy will definitely feel lost when he becomes a father.

Another factor involved could be a mother who protected her son too much and did everything for him except build in him the concept independence and his future fatherhood. Most likely, she did not foster in him a sense of responsibility to and protection for others.

Considering this background, chances are this man is going to choose a woman who will take things out of his hands instead of teaching him fathering skills. If he does choose such a woman (similar to his mother), he may be unable to express his commitment and goodwill toward helping to raise a child. He will definitely feel frustrated because he will be unable to develop a solid relationship with his children. On the other hand, his children will miss the opportunity to experience a good relationship with that loving father who fails due to lack of knowledge.

What can we do about him? What can he do about his environment? Everything. I feel hopeful about this type of dad because he could be helped by therapy if his family is patient and supportive. All it takes to start the healing process is admitting that he needs the help and submitting voluntarily to that help. So it is with the ignorant father. Offer him the help and the training, and you will see wonders.

I admire the modern tendency of obstetricians, clinics, and pediatricians to involve fathers in preconception and prebirth courses. Fathers are encouraged to educate themselves in the whole process of a child's development, and it is amazing how someone who never had the information, modeling, and programming necessary to be a good father can become knowledgeable and involved. If the wife reinforces that feeling, the ignorant but willing father will really fulfill his role happily and successfully.

A Father with Limited Commitment

"You're done when they reach eighteen" is the kind of advice young men hear from other men who want to warn them away from fatherhood. Fatherhood is portrayed as more of a threat than a promise, as if raising a child were a punishment.

Where did this attitude come from? From the legislative and judicial systems, which deem anyone over the age of eighteen an adult and thereby completely responsible for taking care of himself or herself. From this legal designation, many people have derived the idea that after the age of eighteen, a child no longer requires a parent's help, and especially not financial support. Before then, however, in some people's opinions, a parent—most especially a father, for some reason—is doomed to a life of monetary enslavement to his children.

Unfortunately, many men take this advice about fatherhood to heart. When their children turn eighteen they tell them, "You're on your own." But they don't stop to consider how *they* behaved when they were that age. At eighteen, were they mature, experienced, wise? Were they earning enough to live independently? Did they have good judgment? Could they afford an education so that they could provide for a household?

I don't think any of that is likely because, though these men might have enjoyed an abundance of intelligence, they lacked experience and wisdom. At eighteen, no matter who you are or where you're from, major life changes and relevant decisions await you. Will you continue your education, or work, or both? Will you marry and have a family? Even though the legal system considers eighteen-year-olds adults, the truth is that they still need their parents' help. The limited-commitment father, however, has his mind made up that when his kid's eighteen, he—the father—will finally be free.

If we make a reality check, nobody is an adult until he or she is capable of providing for himself and his family, at least decently, without government help. If you are not a born genius like Steve Jobs, Bill Gates, Mark Zuckerberg, or any of those not-so-many men who turned millionaires by themselves, you should have a degree beyond high school in this competitive world.

The Expressionless Father

An expressionless father never shares his emotions—not in his actions, not in his speech, not even in his looks. His children never know if he is disapproving or pleased, if he is going to say "yes" or "no." His reluctance to give them any indication of what he's thinking leaves them with feelings of insecurity and distrust.

An expressionless father is an absent father because he withholds himself from his children. Though he is with them physically day in and day out, they are unable to relate to him; they do not feel loved, and they're not sure what to expect. Nor do they know how they are supposed to behave. Given that this is the only male role model they know in their youth, they might be sadly doomed to copy their father's behavior as adults. And if they relate to their families the same way, they will have unstable and unhappy families.

The Couple-Oriented Father

This type of father is more common than people are willing to accept. What would you think if I told you that men, by nature, are all couple-oriented and not family-oriented? That's the way it is! When a couple-oriented man likes a woman and loves her enough to propose, he is thinking about her and not about raising a family. That is one of the reasons it takes so much for men to deal with the hassles of fatherhood.

However, some men know that they are heading toward having a family of their own, and at the proper moment, they deal with it responsibly. Others do not come to terms with the idea and stick to their couple-oriented mind-sets.

There are correlational possibilities that may explain why this happens:

1- **Being raised as an only child.** In some instances, a guy raised as an only child is used to having all the attention at home and wants to keep it that way. He would consider children as competitors for his wife's attention. This is not a healthy outlook; such an individual is not mature enough to understand that his marital relationship should have nothing to do with his parent-child relationship.

2- **Sticking to the illusion of being forever single.** This guy has not come to terms with his responsibilities as an adult. He considers his wife a partner with whom he can behave like a single man, spending, partying, and building up a future but without the responsibility or financial burden of raising a family.

3- **Past vicarious experiences.** Lots of men have seen couples (very close to them, even their own parents) whose relationships have been torn apart, and their children were blamed for it. Although raising a family is a challenge for some couples more than others, it is unfair to blame the children; it is all about the strength and the adaptive capabilities of the couple. However, these men do not see it that way, and they really think children can jeopardize a couple's relationship.

4- **Lack of commitment and responsibility.** Even if these are underlying factors in all behaviors already described, they may be the main factors in some men. They want the woman but not the whole family package because that may tie them up or commit them for the rest of their lives. They are not ready for a family, and chances are they will never be ready.

The couple-oriented father thinks of his marriage only in terms of himself and his wife, not as a unit from which a happy family can spring. He is happy when he is the sole focus of his wife's attention, and he knows that bringing a child into the picture will destroy that. He cares only for his own happiness, even though there is a child in the household. None of his plans—daily, short-term, long-term—take the child into account, and he shows no interest in the child whatsoever. He attempts again and again to divert his wife's attention toward him as if the child doesn't exist. This is nothing but extreme and unreasonable jealousy.

This type of father is going to be impatient, intolerant, detached, and emotionally absent. Mom will be in full-time charge of the children, who will grow up feeling rejected by the father and extremely attached to their mother, especially as their protector.

As children tend to think that they are to blame for everything around them, they will grow with a guilt not even they understand. The chances of their developing a healthy relationship with their fathers are negligible, not to mention the emotional, psychological, and sometimes physical abuse that they might suffer. This kind of behavior can imprint on a child; it becomes normal to them. Children then risk repeating the pattern in their adult life and spending all their lives reenacting the same drama.

The Father with Severe Mental Issues

Most fathers with severe mental issues never seek professional help, though they could benefit from it. In their minds, however, why should they? They are okay. Many men operate under the delusion that real men don't ask for help, and so their psychiatric issues remain untreated—to the detriment of themselves and everyone around them.

Psychotic fathers come in many forms. Their pathologies might be subtle or blatant and might manifest occasionally or with terrifying frequency. A family may conceal a psychotic father's behavior out of embarrassment or fear, and society, which still frowns on men seeking professional help, can keep him from even trying to help himself. Unfortunately for these families, there is no way to establish a healthy relationship with a psychotic father.

There is a defense mechanism that is even more damaging in dealing with this father: denial. First, not everybody can discern or understand what constitutes a psychotic person. As incredible at it sounds, when bizarre behavior comes into the house, the shock can be so harsh that women try to justify it as a temporary situation. And children either blame themselves or think of it as "normal" because it is what they can relate to.

Most families with psychotic fathers try to deny the situation. If it is finally recognized, the fear can be paralyzing. The mother, who is supposed to be the protective adult, is involved in codependent behavior and denial.

The family members can be so confused that they cannot see from the inside what is obvious to people on the outside. And even if they see it and seek help, they are impotent when they crash into the HIPAA law. According to it, authorities tell her that if the guy does not accept treatment, she cannot make him do it.

When trying to deal with a psychotic father, a child has only two terrible choices: play along and compromise his or her own mental health, or run away and attempt to save himself or herself.

What kind of choice is that? What can these children do? If their father's sanity is compromised and their mother, undoubtedly, is struggling to make up for his absence, who will save the children from getting stuck in the cycle? If they are not rescued, who knows what type of fathers and mothers they will turn out to be?

Unfortunately, most of the time, children who live with psychotic fathers are not rescued; nobody swoops in to save them. Instead, they live powerless in the shadow of their father's illness and rarely grow up to have healthy relationships. There are not even realistic laws to save them, foresee their future families, and break the vicious cycle.

The Lesson

If you're reading this, then you have some interest in parenthood. Whether you're a man or a woman, whether you have children now or are thinking of having some in the future, you must take account of yourself as honestly and openly as you can to prepare yourself to raise them as best as you can.

Consider:

- If you're a man, what kind of father are you, or what kind of father do you want to be?
- If you're a woman, how is your children's father behaving? If you're not married, what kind of father do you think your boyfriend will make after you get married?

If you are a man and you might have children—no matter what commitment level your relationship is at right now—you must keep in mind that fatherhood is a gift and a privilege. To prepare yourself for it, you must not only identify your strengths and weaknesses but also observe and learn from the behaviors of the other men around you. If you have mental-health issues, make the changes you need to and remedy them before you commit to starting a family.

If you are a woman in a relationship with a man who exhibits any of the issues discussed in this chapter, identify them now and do not ignore them. Hold him accountable for his behavior. If he will not step up and try to do better, he is not the right man for you. Run for your life!

Chapter 5

WHAT IT MEANS TO BE A FATHER

"You're the best father ever!"

That's a phrase that every dad wants to hear from his children, especially during the tough teen years. But he doesn't want to hear it just because he lets his kids do whatever they want. He wants them to say it because he treats them with respect and is there for them when they need him.

So how can he do that? How can a man support his kids not just financially but emotionally and also give their mother the time and assistance she needs as well? And how can Mom help him with this process? Raising kids is tough work, no matter how much you love them, and sharing the responsibilities can make life much easier for everyone involved. Cooperative parenting brings peace of mind—and it all starts with the man figuring out what makes him a father.

And that is really where we must look first: at the word *man*. It takes a man—not a *male*—to be a father. A man is an adult who commits to his responsibilities, develops his abilities to their full potential, relates graciously to people, and manages his finances wisely. And he does all this without giving in to or getting derailed by the setbacks we all experience. Life is a series of setbacks and new beginnings; it is dynamic, changing, and uncertain. Raising children is no different, and a man will be ready to rise to the challenge of fatherhood and family.

A man also has firm values, knows right from wrong, has grounded priorities, and knows that he has to work to provide for himself and his family. He gets involved and commits himself completely to the challenging and rewarding enterprise of raising children. He knows that in order to reap, he must first sow, and that building a healthy, happy family requires an investment of his time, energy, and love.

He can have fun along the way, of course, and take every opportunity to enjoy the time he spends with his loved ones. He has many reasons to feel proud and happy and does so on a regular basis. But as a father, he knows that there is a price to be paid for it all. He understands that if he wants the joy that a family can bring, he must give up his selfish behaviors and pursuits. A true man does not mind doing so.

Finding the Balance

Does being a father sound difficult? It can be at times. Is any man capable of fulfilling all that fatherhood requires? Sure! Many men jump into fatherhood with a sense of joy and conviction, eager not only to experience the happiness that having children can bring but also to prove their own reliability. Learning and practicing the principles of fatherhood is a lot of work, and a lot of people these days want only what comes easily. Some men react irresponsibly even to the possibility of fatherhood. Other men get scared and anxious, but the emotional reward they feel helps them cope with their new reality as fathers.

Fatherhood is a serious matter. Like every other aspect of life, it requires balance to work as it's supposed to. Yes, being a father entails changing diapers and contributing to the family's financial picture. But it also calls for sharing with children some less-tangible things such as knowledge, love, humor, and fun. When a man can balance what his family needs with what they want from him—and deliver it all with patience and grace—then he can truly call himself a father.

However, it really starts much earlier than that. A father is born when he starts dating the woman he is planning to marry. Of course, at that point, he usually isn't thinking about family at all, but his method of courtship, his manners, and his behavior toward his lady and his immediate family all signify the sense of fatherhood he has.

Courtship needs to be the beginning of fatherhood because a good father should first be a good partner. The couple is the foundation of the family, and the father must be involved in every aspect of the household long before any baby arrives. The couple should establish good teamwork, or a division of labor, before having children. They will need this foundation once they start building their family.

If a couple hasn't learned how to work as a team, then they are in trouble when baby comes along. Raising children is a test of patience and can push a relationship to the breaking point, but with some planning and an understanding that life will be radically different with a baby in the house, a man and a woman can work together to make things more manageable, even magical.

The best thing a man can do toward this end is to not assume he is less qualified to raise children than his wife is. When it comes to children, men are generally scared of doing something wrong, especially with newborns. And too many women play into those fears by taking over childrearing completely. Instead of dividing the labor, women throw themselves into the role of solitary caregiver, tending to all the baby's needs and leaving Dad with little to do.

What the mother *should* do is get the father engaged early and often, to allow him to make mistakes, learn, and eventually grow into his role. Mothers, let your husbands screw up—and when they do, show them patience and give them support. They'll be clumsy; they'll hold the baby wrong and act as if they don't know which end of the diaper is up. But you have to let them put one— or two, or three—on wrong in order for them to learn how to do it. Give them a chance. Remember, they are not taught to play with dolls or play house, but they eventually get it right.

Decisions, Decisions

Before a couple even gets to parenthood, they must sit down and make some decisions together. When should they have a baby? What must they do to prepare for it? A woman might feel that these responsibilities fall squarely on her shoulders, but it's essential that she involve the father-to-be in this process. She will be the bearer, but he is more than a mere donor. She should treat him like the father she wants him to be, and more than likely he will rise to the occasion. We as a society have just come to expect that he won't—and have given him a pass when he hasn't. Now's the time to push back against that irresponsible mind frame and get our men involved.

When a man first learns that his wife or girlfriend is pregnant, he will most likely be filled with tremendous emotions: fear that he won't be a good father, worry that something will happen to his child, concern that he won't be able to provide for his family, and, of course, the joy that comes from bringing a new life into the world. His wife or girlfriend is suddenly no longer just his companion and lover; she is the mother of his child, and that alone is reason to celebrate.

Women, it is your job as his partner to help him navigate these feelings and come out of them with a positive perspective. Instead of reaffirming his latent fear that he will not be good enough, you must reassure him that he will excel as a father—as long as you work as a team to prepare yourselves for parenthood.

By the time you become pregnant, your man should know that he'll be expected to support you through every aspect of it—that means being around for the entire forty weeks of gestation, not just as an observer, but as a knowledgeable and joyful participant. Your significant other should know more about the whole process of pregnancy than anybody else because his job begins at conception, not at birth.

Expecting the Baby

When it comes to having a child, women, obviously, bear the majority of the life-building duties. They deal with the day-to-day physical changes of pregnancy for nine months and give birth to the child. But a mother-to-be should never think that her ownership of the process means that her husband doesn't have to be involved.

To help a man become a father, a woman must allow him to be involved in every aspect of pregnancy. He should go to doctor visits as well as birthing and parenting classes, and he should learn and understand the development process that both mother and child are going through together. As the birth nears, he can help paint and furnish the nursery.

This involvement is a critical step in showing your man that he is not just a sperm donor. He has to be engaged, appreciated and encouraged to move into this new phase. Offering this kind of involvement isn't always easy for a woman. Most major celebrations leading up to a baby's birth, such as a shower, are designated as "women only," and men traditionally resist getting closely involved in such events. You don't have to force him to go to a baby shower, of course, but for all possible occasions, he should be by your side. This will help him feel loved and accounted for. The bigger a role he plays in the pregnancy, the more connected he will feel to his child.

Welcome, Baby—and Beyond

After the baby is born, Daddy should be there, involved and helping. As the father—a serious, meaningful job title if ever there was one—it is his duty to be aware of every detail of his baby. He must observe his child's behavior; he must understand what its crying means, what makes him or her laugh, the ins and outs of the baby's feeding schedule. The father must work diligently to create an early and ongoing bond with his son or daughter through touch and voice, through being present for physical interaction. He must also be eager to assist with the baby's needs.

With a good father, this concern and interest will not wane as the baby grows. A good father makes sure to stay involved and informed in all aspects of his child's life. He knows the pediatrician personally and has introduced himself to the people at the day care. An involved father should be a familiar face to the people who take part in his child's life. He is part of a team now—he is its co-captain. Opting out at this point is simply not an option for him.

When the child enters school, it's more important than ever for the father to be protective of his son or daughter and aware of his or her activities and schedule. At school, your child is on his or her own, away from parental supervision. A father must do whatever he can to stay involved, from helping to build that model of the solar system to attending PTA meetings. The teachers of a child with a good father know they can count on him to support their efforts to nurture the child. And when school isn't going so well, a good father will be there for that, too.

The First Months

The beginning of a child's life is a lot of work. It's also the culmination of the parents' preparatory efforts. Encourage your child's father to understand the birthing process and what will happen to your body as you go into labor. Some men might balk at the idea of talking about the birthing process, but encourage him to take an active role and know how his child will come into the world.

When you get to the hospital, the father should go with you into the delivery room and be present when the baby is born. If you have a C-section, your partner should be present for that as well, unless the doctors advise otherwise.

Witnessing the birth will solidify his place in the child's life from the very beginning. He will cherish forever the memory of seeing his child enter the world and boast to his friends about his new baby boy or girl.

Once the baby is born, the real work begins. The first months of a child's life can turn into a major test for any marriage. Some new parents might resent their babies because they require feeding or diaper changing every few hours, which can seriously cut into the parents' sleeping schedules. Some might lament their newly limited freedom—no more spontaneous trips or lazy evenings at the movies. The baby is now the center of their world, and everything they do must defer to the new presence in their lives.

No one is prepared to be a father or a mother. Women usually have more childcare experience because they have more likely been called on to babysit, but that's different from taking care of a baby around the clock. Even though other parents and family members might have tried to help you get ready, you can't be. In your fifth month of no sleep, you'll understand.

Before the baby arrives, the parents-to-be should work out a schedule for nighttime responsibilities. It will be great if your partner doesn't work the first two weeks after the baby is born so that he can fully immerse himself in the experience. The most important thing during this stressful time is teamwork. Get the father to take on some of the night shifts. It will help you, and it will give him a chance to learn how to care for the baby by himself. Midnight feedings and diaper changes can help build a bond between father and child. Even if you're breastfeeding and need to be up each time the baby's hungry, your partner can get up to change a diaper or assist with anything else that needs to be done.

During these first few months, stress can build in one or both partners. It helps for each to have some time away from the baby, either with friends or alone. Create schedules, and be prepared to make some compromises. There are many ways to deal with the tension, but how to do so should be worked out beforehand and not improvised.

When a baby comes along, romance in a marriage can take a major hit. A new father needs to be reassured that he is still important, still desirable, and still a focus in his woman's life. However, he must be aware of the effects of postpartum blues and not take it personally if his wife seems less than affectionate sometimes. The more emotional support a new mother gets at this stage, the sooner the couple will be able to restore their regular marital relationship. Physical touch is very important and a great way to show love.

The father should be more adept at his new role in life after a couple months of on-the-job training. He should be able to read the baby's signals—for example, to tell if the baby is hungry or has a dirty diaper. During his overnight shifts he will have learned how to soothe the baby and put him or her back down to bed. By being involved in his child's early life, he has made it easier to maintain a strong connection with his child later in life. They have gone through something together, and now the father knows what it takes to help his child thrive.

Listening and Learning

As his son or daughter goes through the stages of childhood, a good, present father is, above all else, supportive and protective of his or her feelings and needs. A father must listen to his child when he or she has something to say, but even beyond that, he must be attuned to his child's unspoken signals. Kids can't always articulate what they're feeling, so both parents need to listen carefully to figure out what's wrong. Being accessible—sometimes simply offering a kid a shoulder to cry on—will be among a father's biggest jobs.

In addition to listening, however, a father has to dish out advice. The key here is to make sure the words of wisdom are on the kid's level of understanding; make sure he or she understands not only what you're saying, but *why* you're telling them. Building a foundation of trust and understanding is important because, even though being a dad comes before being a friend, you don't want to come across as a dictator. Know when to say "yes" and when to say "no" and do so firmly. Your child will respect you for both.

Always Learning

Of course, no man is born knowing how to be a good father. He must put in the work it takes to become one, and much of that comes simply from *doing*. As a father raises his kids, he learns how to guide and lead them, and that takes time and patience. Frustration is as much a part of raising kids as the happiness and joy it brings, but a father must control his anger and demonstrate to his kids what it means to be patient, kind, and respectful.

Kids learn behaviors through modeling, and if a father is firm but understanding, chances are his boy or girl will be the same with his or her children one day. And that is the positive cycle we want to create.

When a father does make a mistake and loses his cool, it's on his shoulders to acknowledge it and apologize to his children. Though kids are supposed to do what their parents tell them to, they're not robots—sometimes they'll do things you don't want them to. And when they do, remember that they are your children, your flesh and blood, and they deserve to be treated with respect, just as you wish to be. It's easy to blow up or yell when your child breaks something or talks back. What's difficult is slowing down, thinking about what has happened, and then formulating an appropriate response.

None of us are going to do that 100 percent of the time. Sometimes we will blow up. But a good parent—and especially a good father—will recognize his own mistakes and use them as learning experiences for himself and his children. Doing this takes courage; it's not easy to admit that you're wrong, especially when you're an authority figure. But if you're going to help your children grow up, you have to grow up yourself. A good dad knows that and embraces opportunities to learn from mistakes and move past them. With this behavior, kids learn to accept their mistakes, apologize, and make up for them.

Modeling this kind of measured behavior is especially important for boys because they need to be shown not only that making mistakes and learning slowly are valuable, but that it's okay—and even good and desirable—for fathers to play an integral part in childrearing. Many boys are led to believe from an early age that they have no business taking care of children; the first time they hold a baby of a family member, for instance, they are mocked because they are timid, afraid to hurt the young child. Instead, they should be shown the correct way to interact with a baby and encouraged to keep trying and learning—just as their own fathers had to.

Being a father is a balancing act. A dad who wants to be a major part of his children's lives must be supportive, present, and available, but he can't be too easy on them because it's his responsibility to make sure that they grow to be good people who treat others with respect. It seems like a tall order—and on some days, it really is—but as long as Dad keeps learning and growing himself, he will constantly improve his relationship with his kids and ensure that they will grow up to be the best they can be.

The Lesson

Childrearing is a full-time job. You don't raise a child correctly by chance. No, you make long-term *and* short-term plans, all while maintaining the flexibility to deal with unexpected events— which happen more frequently than you can imagine, and at any age your child might be.

Raising a child is an exercise in mental gymnastics. To be a good parent, you must develop predictive abilities and stay ahead of your children's thoughts—in other words, you should know better than they know and do better than they do. Parenthood is certainly unpredictable, but you can make it easier on everyone involved by setting up a foundation ahead of time. Know what you and your partner's commitments to your children are and make the important decisions. What you do at the start can determine what kind of parent you will be.

Chapter 6

SEXUAL FREEDOM AND FATHERHOOD

Three generations ago, when I was growing up in Puerto Rico, there were fathers in most families—and all of them were respected. Sometimes it was out of fear, which was not good, but more often it was out of simple respect for the position. And that is the attitude we're after.

Traditionally, the paternal role encompassed financial support and protection. It also involved defending the honor of the family, and that included ensuring that any young couple who found themselves in a family way owned up to their responsibilities. Let's say a young man got his girlfriend pregnant. If he came from a family with a good male role model, he had only two options: coerced or free-will marriage. Either way, he would not question the fact that he had to take care of that woman and their child. If it was for a lifetime or not, time would tell, but everybody assumed that the child had to be born under the protection of marriage and the honor of the woman had to be protected.

Today, however, sexual freedom and a lack of good role models have brought on sexual irresponsibility and a lack of respect for values and life. Women of all ages get pregnant, and their guys go on with their lives as if nothing has happened. In many instances, women just go along with that attitude and even foster it. We praise single mothers all the time for the burdens they carry, as if it's a more honorable situation than raising a child with a father. And we have two types of single mothers: the one who is abandoned by her mate and the one who does not want to get married just because she is pregnant and even refuses the presence of her child's father.

Don't get me wrong—single mothers deserve to be recognized and helped. Raising a child (or children) alone is tough. However, in deifying single mothers, we have come to treat men as mere sperm donors. This is humiliating—they are, after all, people with feelings and deserve to be treated as such—but it is also very convenient for the men. It allows them to get out of the responsibility of raising the children they conceive.

So many women view men as unnecessary in the procreation process once it gets past sex that some even turn to scientific methods to get the job done: artificial insemination or in-vitro fertilization using donated sperm. In such a situation, there is no relationship, no sharing, no emotional risk-taking. These women are sure they do not need men by their sides and so opt for a controlled, predictable, and easier method of choosing a father for their children. It's a struggle to find the right man in the singles scene, but there's always the hope of finding one who wants to get married and have kids.

But cutting the father out of the children's lives from the very beginning sets the children up for a lifetime of issues. They will wonder why their father is not present and maybe spend the rest of their lives looking for a replacement, most of the time unconsciously. If they are girls, this could lead to a string of dysfunctional relationships; boys will look for the role models they never had in any man who gives them attention, no matter how morally questionable.

But let's not put all the focus here on those mothers who choose to be single. There are also what I call *married* single mothers. These women also consider their husbands mere sperm donors. The men have no clue about sharing the joy of raising children or being part of a family—nor do they want one. Now, I am sure that men do not like to be regarded only as sperm donors. They are, after all, people with self-esteem and self-respect. The problem, then, is that so many of them are unprepared for the role. So, how do you get a man to be a father? Let's take a look at the different stages of preparation.

Dating

When men and women are dating, they usually focus on the chemistry and the so-often-used phrase "falling in love." Women are romantically inclined and tend to get swept up in the glow of a passionate relationship. Men are often more couple- or sex-oriented. Neither party really thinks about long-term relationship maintenance. Both believe that if there is great chemistry, a long-term relationship has a good chance of succeeding. After all, passion and romance are the keys to a happy life together, right?

Wrong! While chemistry is important, it's not enough to sustain a long-term relationship that will one day produce children. Being married and raising children together involves a lot of teamwork, respect, and patience. A relationship has to be able to withstand the stresses of childrearing. But these things are rarely at the forefront of how women and men think about their partners.

Today, as far as women are concerned, dating is more about marketing than honest discussion. Does he have the right car and the right clothes? Does he make enough money to support her lifestyle? Can they buy the big house? Will she look good on his arm? Such a window-shopping woman fails to look at the man in front of her as a future husband or father—as someone who will share in family responsibilities day after day. She sees him only as a nice smile, a strong arm around her, or maybe even simply a wallet.

If a woman doesn't look at how a man deals with children, what his relationship with his family is like, and how supportive he is during tough times, she might never see what her future husband is really like. Romance is great, but once the bloom is off the rose, the real work starts, and that's when a husband and father succeeds or fails. If women aren't thinking about these things while dating, then their men certainly aren't either. And if no one's considering the future, then there can't be much hope for success in the long run.

To build a foundation that will lead to a happy, functional family down the road, a woman has to be mature enough when she starts dating to notice if the relationship is going seriously. She must ask herself: Is this a man I could marry? Is our relationship about more than just romance? Is he going to be a good father? Then she must answer these questions honestly. Often, a woman is so oriented toward motherhood that she believes she can raise kids on her own as long as her man provides money, but this is a fallacy, and it is not the only option she has. She must recognize and act upon her man's potential ability to support her and their children emotionally.

If a woman who wants children discovers that her man isn't going to be a good father, then she should leave him, as it's clear that she won't have a good future with him. But as we all know, this is easier said than done. To prevent having to make this sort of decision, a woman needs to think first and then fall in love. She must decide ahead of time which qualities she wants in a partner, and not just for right now, but long-term, when he will become her husband and the father of their children. She must think about how she wants her children treated and what kind of man would treat them that way. She should consider how well she works with her man and if she could equally divide the labor of raising a family with him.

If you catch yourself falling in love without considering these issues first, then slow down. Love will make you live in denial about a man's flaws as a potential father. If you allow that to happen, you will be setting yourself up for a lot of heartache down the line. Your man might look charming, but take off those sunglasses. You need to decide if he's going to be a good father.

To do this, first look at his relationship with his family. If he's good with them, then chances are he'll be a good father. If he didn't have a good relationship with his father, don't automatically count him out—he can still make an effort to be a great dad himself.

Next, pay attention to how he treats you. Does he have patience? Is he generous and respectful? Does he have irrational outbursts? Is he financially wise or is he a big spender? What are his priorities in life? What about his friends? Are they good, respectful family men? How a man behaves toward his friends says a lot about his concepts of loyalty and how well he manages the ups and downs of relationships.

If those areas of a man's life are in order, then you are off to a good start. Don't be afraid to ask him what he thinks of fatherhood and childrearing. He might feel like you're pressuring him—some men, having been discouraged their whole lives from becoming fathers, view any such questioning almost as accusations. But for your sake, it's better to find out his views on these matters before, rather than after, a child is born.

During the courtship phase and beyond, there is plenty of time for romance. And you should take advantage of that—it's half the fun. But don't let it completely take over. You have to find out while you're dating whether your boyfriend is really the one for you. Once you have a child with him, you can't replace him. Our society encourages women to stand on their own and make it through life no matter what the setbacks, but raising children should be a team effort, and finding a good teammate needs to start before the first romantic gaze. A woman should decide ahead of time what she wants for her kids and make that a priority as she's being swept off her feet.

But, you might ask, why is all of this up to the women? Because men are short-term thinkers. They are very couple-oriented during the dating phase and think mostly of their relationship as it stands in any given moment. Some men do think about family and marriage, but unless they have been shown how important their role as a father will be, they don't usually express their desire for these things to the women they date. In fact, talk of family and marriage is a quick way to scare a lot of men. But it really does need to be discussed if the relationship is getting serious.

The Lesson

Have fun during courtship. It is a very important part of the relationship, and that time will never come back as it is. But keep in mind all the time that dating and courtship are a marketing stage. Both of you are "selling" yourselves as "the best product," and chances are, neither of you is being completely honest about your virtues and shortcomings. If you are planning on a serious relationship, be straightforward about asking those questions you may be afraid to ask even if you are not sure you want to hear the answers. The answers may finish the relationship, or they may enhance it. If they finish it, the relationship was not the one you were looking for. If the answers are music to your ears, your chances are good that you have found a good father for your children. Is it worth the risk?

Chapter 7

THE GREAT FALSE MYTH: ARE FATHERS REPLACEABLE?

Because there are so many absentee fathers in our society, thousands of women have had to adapt to life without them. Because so many biological fathers have refused to—or been barred from—taking active roles in raising their children, many women have decided that they can raise children on their own or find a good man to take the place of the biological father.

In fact, according to a National Fatherhood Initiative study titled "Mama Says: A National Survey of Mothers' Attitudes of Fathers and Fatherhood," most mothers think that Dad is replaceable! Which is strange, because 93 percent of moms surveyed said that they believe there is a father-absence crisis. If dads are a dime a dozen, why are women so disturbed by men who run away from them? Probably because fathers are *not* replaceable. Of course, sometimes, women have very good reasons to believe that their lives and the lives of their children will be better without the father's involvement—specifically in cases of abuse. No woman should stay in an abusive relationship or expose her children to a man who can't control his anger. But barring the case of abusive fathers, children will generally be better off with their biological fathers in their lives.

In some cultures, there is a belief that this isn't true—and that while there's only one mother, anyone can be a father. But this is a myth that has been proven false time and again. Just look at the fallout children experience when they realize their biological fathers won't be involved in raising them.

The Value of Being There

Abandonment is powerful and destructive. Even if children have the support of a loving mother and a good, caring man, they tend to feel guilty because their biological father has left them. They feel as though they did something to push their father away, as if they weren't good enough to keep him in the home, or as if they did not deserve Dad's love. Everyone wants to feel loved, and love means acceptance. If you aren't accepted by the man who gave you life, how are you ever supposed to know what love is?

Nothing can replace the bond—spiritual and mental and emotional—between a father and his biological children. Watching his child grow inside his partner strikes a chord deep inside a man; it makes him realize that together they have created a miracle. This realization then instills in him a vested interest in the well-being of his child. A good father will go to great lengths to make sure that he or she is safe and supported.

A good father will also realize that the mother of his children needs support and care not only during the pregnancy, but after as well. Many men are extremely attendant to their wives during pregnancy but then forget about her when the child is born. Instead of helping take care of both, they become jealous and demanding because they have to share Mom's time with the newborn. Being a great father *and* a great husband means being vigilant when it comes to the emotional and mental state of the mother.

Rotating Fathers

Though many children have found great role models in stepfathers and adoptive parents, more commonly they grow attached to men their mothers bring into their lives and then suffer feelings of abandonment if those men eventually leave. If a single mother is actively dating, she will likely bring a man home to meet her children at some point if she feels the relationship is serious. Should she date a man for a year or more, her children might grow attached to him and even benefit from having a good man in their lives. But if the relationship then fails, the children will be left feeling as though they have done something wrong or that this new father figure has left because of them.

Because of this, a mother must always look critically at the adult relationships she forms. When they end, even if it's on good terms, they can greatly affect the development of her children. Eventually, children can grow resentful of their mother's relationships or of any new man she brings into the home. Daughters might become distrustful of men in general, believing they will never find one who will stick around forever. Many women raised in the absence of their biological fathers never come to trust men—or go the opposite way and trust too many in a doomed attempt to find the connection they lost so long before.

Sons often become protective of their mothers and try to assume the role of husband and protector in the household when no father figure is there to do it for him. Such boys, even though they might be quite young, are only doing what they think is right and what comes naturally to many males. But this protective instinct leaves its own scars. These boys have a great deal of built-up, internalized anger, and they harden themselves to the world, believing they can trust no one.

Later in life, this anger and resentment can manifest in the form of criminal or even abusive behavior. Such men look for women who are like their mothers and take out their frustrations on them; if they aren't abusive, often they're simply overprotective. These men project the emotions from their childhoods onto the situations in their new homes and figuratively suffocate their spouses and children by denying them freedom.

A Dangerous Mistake

Many men feel that if they leave their wives or girlfriends after the birth of a child, the woman can replace them as fathers and partners and everybody will be okay after a while. They often believe this because of their own upbringings or because of the influence of their families—especially the women, who believe that men are unnecessary beyond conception and pass this attitude down to their sons, nephews, and grandsons.

Unfortunately, all this does is give the boys raised in such environments an excuse—a way out of their responsibility. This does a great disservice to these boys, who will one day be men with families of their own. If, at that point, they believe that they are worthless and unnecessary to the childrearing process, how can they be expected to want to participate in it?

In reality, of course, we know that men are just as necessary as women. To reinforce this, families should show their boys how powerful the influence of a good father can be. Mothers, sisters, and aunts should tell their boys that men are as central to families as women are, even in matriarchal societies in which women make most of the decisions. Men should still be there to influence and support those decisions.

Be a Parent, Not a Friend

Single parents tend to think of their children as friends. The children are the only people in their lives, the only ones with whom they share a deep bond, and of course, they want to make their children happy. So many single parents spoil their children—and end up with kids who lack discipline and act resentful when they should be thankful.

Under all circumstances, a parent is a parent. You might behave like a friend or a confidante if the necessity arises, if your son or daughter comes to you for advice or consolation. But day to day, a child simply needs a parent and what that means: safety, protection, wisdom, life experience, authority, unconditional love, the best advice that works for his or her best interests, reliability, and support. That unique relationship should never be replaced.

The Lesson

A father's abandonment can affect a child for life. A father is supposed to be there through thick and thin; when he's not, his children suffer—and so does he. As long as a man is mentally healthy, when he has children, he must fulfill the role of father; he must be held responsible and encouraged to complete his duties to the best of his abilities. A woman must support her man in this endeavor—and in return, he must support her as she bears and delivers their children, and even beyond.

The role of father has been marginalized in our society by those who view parenting as a part-time job, as something to be shared only with the staff at the day care center. To make our dads understand their own importance, we must begin by making it clear that no one can take their place.

Chapter 8

MAKE IT LEGAL

If you want to bring a child into the world, you should first have a home with stability and structure. Legal marriage provides these things more than most couples might think.

When a man marries a woman, he takes a vow to protect her and their family. He shows a commitment that goes beyond simply living with the mother of his children. He promises that he will stick it out for better or worse, for richer or poorer, in sickness and in health.

Of course, it isn't guaranteed that a man will do these things simply because he has married the mother of his children. Many absentee fathers are married and living in the family home. Marriage isn't just about making vows. It is a sign of a man's legal commitment to his children and spouse. When he takes the step of making his relationship official, he is going beyond the act of moving into a house or an apartment. He is stating to his woman, to his children (present or future), and to the world that he is ready to take responsibility.

And a woman should demand this commitment before agreeing to have his children. She should express to her man that marriage is important and that his presence in the home means something. She should show him that he's appreciated and that she wants him to raise his children with her in the sanctity of marriage.

Some question the effect a traditional marriage can have on the health of the children it produces. Many critics of the institution of marriage say that a couple can live together and love each other and be good parents to their children. This is true. But in reality such couples are not common.

As mentioned in Chapter One, millions of American children are living without fathers, and that number is likely to grow. Studies have shown time and time again that married fathers are more supportive of and have closer relationships with their children and that they offer benefits that other family members cannot.

According to a Center for Marriage and Families report published in 2006, African-American boys are less likely than boys in the general public to excel academically, more likely to get in trouble with the law, and more likely to experience a lower level of well-being. The study found that these results can be attributed to several factors, including a high rate of fatherless homes in the African-American community.

The Center for Marriage and Families also found that when African-American men are married, they are more emotionally supportive and more committed to socializing their children, setting boundaries, disciplining, and helping their children with problems. Black youths whose parents are married and present in the home are more likely to view their fathers as important role models—probably because of the consistent emotional support they receive.

This is just one study among dozens across multiple social groups that have emphasized the importance of marriage. Even things like infant mortality rates, these studies have shown, are lower among married women with committed partners.

In a different study, the Center for Marriage and Families found that marriage was a predictor of happiness and that married couples reported higher levels of psychological well-being, which translates into stability in the home. As a result, children of married couples are less likely to try drugs, less likely to commit crimes, and *five times* less likely to live in poverty. To our concern, a recent statistic revealed that 40 percent of couples living together are not legally married. Will the problem become worse in the near future?

Unfortunately, the number of children being raised in fatherless homes is on the rise. These children make up approximately one-twelfth of our entire population and are unwittingly at the root of many of the country's problems with crime and poverty. In fact, the National Fatherhood Initiative estimates that the United States government spends in the neighborhood of $100 billion per year on anti-poverty efforts and child-support enforcement.

Making It Legal

Despite these alarming statistics, many men and women still believe that living separately or in a union with no official standing is good enough when raising their children. They think that even though they do not present a stable, unified front to their children, they are being good role models—especially the fathers. The NFI found that nonresident dads think they're doing a better job of parenting than the mothers of their children think they are. Maybe that's because most fathers whose partnerships are not official under the law feel less obligated to support their children financially and emotionally. Sure, they created the kids, but as far as they're concerned, that doesn't mean they have to provide for them, so when they do, they think they are doing more than they are supposed to.

While some people argue that marriage is merely a construct of churches and the government and that it provides no guarantee of a loving home, that is just an excuse for evading commitment. In truth, nothing can guarantee a loving home—but a man and a woman can do everything within their power to ensure that the family they create will have the closest thing to it possible. This includes making a legal commitment to one another.

For a man, marriage is a step that indicates a strong willingness to take part in the lives of his children. Many unmarried men will claim that their commitment is total and that they don't need "a piece of paper" to prove that they love their wives and children, but that is simply manipulation on their part. That is avoiding legal marriage and the responsibility it entails. In fact, many men actively avoid marriage because they fear the financial or legal consequences they'll face if it ends in divorce—up to and including paying child support, with the mother's firsthand knowledge of his earnings because they were married. Imagine being afraid to give financial support to your child! Such men sure weren't scared of the fun that led to the creation of that child in the first place.

What it comes down to is this: If a man is so convinced that a marriage certificate will have no bearing on his ability to raise a family, then why *wouldn't* he get married? What difference would it make if he *did* have that little piece of paper?

Time to Choose

When confronted with fatherhood, a man has several choices. First, he can live with his children and their mother and work hard to support them all. Second, he can live elsewhere and avoid supporting them in any way. Third, he can live apart from his family and support them only financially.

Unfortunately, millions of men in this country choose the last two options, and the abundance of nonlegal partnerships today does nothing but encourage them. If he's not "tied down" by a legal marriage, a man feels as though he can walk away at any time with no real repercussions—and often, that instinct is correct.

And what message does that send to his woman? If a man is hesitant to enter into a sanctioned relationship, how much do you think he really wants to be with her? The answer: not much. That's why he keeps that trap door open—in case he needs to make a quick escape.

This is an incredible change in men's attitudes toward marriage. It used to be that men did "the right thing" and married the women they got pregnant. This was no guarantee that they would be perfect husbands and fathers, but it was at least a symbol of commitment—and a reminder that they were responsible for their actions. Getting a woman pregnant used to carry with it a certain level of responsibility for the life of the child.

Today, there is little such responsibility. A man gets a woman pregnant, and "the right thing" can mean anything from suggesting she get an abortion—on him!—to accusing her of trying to set him up. Very rarely do you see a man stepping up to marry the mother of his unplanned child. Even rarer do you see someone holding him accountable for this behavior.

An analogy I like to use is that just as you cannot be *sort of* pregnant, you cannot say that you are committed to someone and then refuse marriage. Either you're in it or you're not; refusal to marry does nothing but give away your true feelings and show that you have reservations about a permanent relationship. Your partner will pick up on that hesitation and realize that the relationship is doomed. If you won't marry, in reality, you have one foot out the door. You're already ready to leave.

The Benefits of Marriage

What men need to learn is that getting legally married is not just about making their girlfriends happy or burdening themselves financially forever. Indeed, marriage can provide a great number of legal protections and benefits to husband, wife, and child that other unions simply cannot.

When it comes to insurance, health-care benefits, maternity leave, family medical leave, power of attorney, school decisions, and more, being legally declared someone's spouse and someone's father can make all the difference. There's a reason gay couples have been fighting for the right to be married: Marriage provides protections that civil unions and unofficial partnerships cannot.

Without the protections of a legal marriage, if the father of a child were to suffer an untimely death, the mother could be left not just without a father for her children but without financial support. If he had any sort of life insurance, pension, or other assets, a woman who is simply a girlfriend will have no legal right to it.

Even if for this reason alone, a man who wants to demonstrate his commitment to his family should take that step and enter a legal marriage. It makes sense on many levels. It demonstrates to his woman that he is determined to do the right thing, even when it means taking a chance that the relationship won't work out, and that he'll be responsible for both her and their children financially.

Learning to Wait

Unfortunately, statistics show that 52 percent of marriages in the United States don't work out. That number scares away a lot of people, and understandably so. It would be ignorant to think that divorce cannot happen. It could happen to you. So what should you do if it does?

Many rocky relationships will work, given more effort, help, time, and commitment. Many, however, will not. I blame this on one of our society's major ailments: desperation for immediate gratification. Today, adults act like small children who haven't learned that good things come to those who wait. They want fun and excitement and enticement around every corner; they want to be constantly stimulated without having to work much for it.

The problem? That's just not how marriage works. In any human relationship, you have to be patient. You must understand that gratification can take a while—days, months, sometimes even years. You must learn the art of negotiation. You sometimes must delay your joy so that your loved ones might have theirs. Marriage, like every human relationship that pretends to endure, is a full-time job. In order to make it easier, the partners need to have common goals and similar points of view on life's main issues, the same priorities and tolerance to changes.

The Argument for Marriage

Men, if you really care about the mothers of your children, and you really feel that you want to be in the family home, supporting your partners and kids, you should enter into an official union. Think about the happy homes you know—those of your family and your friends. Think about the mothers and fathers and their commitment to each other. Those wedding bands they wear symbolize something special—something permanent.

Much of what makes a long-term partnership work is the conscious decision by both members to consider it permanent. If a husband and wife commit to a marriage, the chances of raising a successful, happy family are much higher. A good marriage is a lot of work, but nothing really good is ever really easy. Raising children together and working on being a couple will draw you together and make you stronger in the long run.

The Lesson

Women, if you've dated a man for long enough that you're expecting a marriage proposal, don't settle for anything less. If your boyfriend suggests moving in together with no guarantee of marriage, you're looking at the wrong man for the job of husband and father. Children deserve to be born into the best possible situations for their well-being, and that means having two dedicated, *married* parents who are secure enough in their relationship to make it legal and binding.

In general, I try to respect other people's opinions and decisions. But when a man says that he's not ready to marry you legally or wants to live with you to see if he eventually will marry you, he obviously is not willing to assume responsibility. He does not want to be responsible for you, your relationship, or your children, whether you have them yet or not. And if he feels like this now, after you've dated a while? Chances are he will never be ready. Neither are you ready to waste your time for his convenience.

Chapter 9

CHANGE COMES ONE PERSON AT A TIME

The "textbook" concept of society is still the same. One individual joins another individual, and they form a couple. This couple starts congregating with others until a community is formed, and many communities together are what make up a society. This concept of society then becomes very general.

Problems and situations that were once isolated, pertaining only to the individual, can become *social problems* if too many individuals within society experience them. As soon as they become social problems, this is what happens:

1- Individuals refuse to be held personally responsible for their wrongdoing just because the problem is "social" and the situation is "trendy" and "normal" in our "times of social change."

2- Everybody starts relying on the government to come up with magical solutions, and there is no awareness that if a person has an issue, he, individually, has to address it.

3- Everybody's irresponsible behavior is justified, fostered, and promoted.

4- Since problems turned into behavior are rewarded (reinforced), then the behavior turns into a "social change."

5- When statistics underline the high cost of the behavior, government and society panic.

6- When the government and society finally intervene, they deal with the symptoms but not with the causes.

7- You cannot underestimate the power of denial. When people are brought up a certain way, they really believe their way is the right way to live. It takes a lot of effort to accept that there is an unhealthy situation around.

8- We cannot deny the convenience of saying "times have changed; you know how things are nowadays," which leads people to accept problems as normal ways of contemporary living. Then you are not held responsible for anything.

All this analysis brings us to why the fatherhood issue has to be addressed at the individual level. Problems become social when a significant number of individuals suffer them. That also applies to changes.

Has somebody done the math on how much of the $100 billion that fatherless families are costing us could be saved long-term if we were to introduce a curriculum on parenthood at different levels of understanding according to age, from elementary school through high school? We teach many courses the students never use, but most people's historic reality is that they will become parents some day in life, and the school system should get them ready for that.

The change we need must start of course when our men are not yet men but still boys.

We will address what to do about our current fathers, but lasting improvement means planning for the future, so we begin this chapter with a discussion of how we can educate the young boys in our culture about their future responsibilities as men and fathers.

Beginning with Mom

Education of any kind begins in the home. When a boy is raised without a father, he is influenced by what he sees in his own home: a single parent and a missing father. He is shown a "normal" family life that is anything but. While this type of home is less than optimal, we don't have to waste the opportunity to use the situation to rally ourselves and to push for greater responsibility.

Our single mothers (and mothers living with absentee fathers) must make a choice to use their situations for good; to teach their sons and daughters the tremendous responsibility that comes with being a parent. But they can't teach what they don't know. That means they need help educating their kids, and that is where we as a society can help.

Many single mothers are let down by a system that teaches them nothing about living as a good parent or about selecting a good husband and father. Since we cannot depend on our families to teach these things, the creation of social programs that teach and support single mothers will go a long way toward showing them that they are not *supposed* to be alone and that their husbands or boyfriends are in fact wrong for not taking part in the raising of their children.

We have myriad social programs that support women financially and provide job training and day care. But we have few social programs that provide modeling for these young women. And by *modeling,* I mean demonstrating what a whole familial unit can look like and how it can operate in every way: daily living, financially, and emotionally.

Many of our mothers are living with absentee fathers and don't know what a good husband and father is supposed to act like or what they should be asking of their spouses. Programs that supply financial or medical assistance are wonderful, but not all of our Supermoms need money. Many of them just need some assistance in "seeing" what their husbands are not doing.

Our single mothers are often the products of fatherless homes. Without a break in the cycle, they will continue to pass on the attitudes and biases that landed them in the same situations as their own mothers.

Pushing Dad

We start by refusing to accept the current behavior. While it is true that each person must modify his or her own behavior, social pressures can make people change their ways. Forty years ago, if a man left his wife or girlfriend and child to fend for themselves, he would be shunned. Today we accept it as all too normal. What if we stopped?

It's obviously a fine line between standing up for a principle and meddling in someone's private life. But as a society, we have put pressure on people in order to change offensive behaviors.

The "politically correct" movement has made it unacceptable to use racist or misogynist language in most workplaces and in public. And while this movement may not have changed the internal views of many, it has certainly raised awareness about how harmful racist language can be.

If we can initiate a program of similar prevalence and pressure in order to tout the benefits of good fathering, we can make real changes in the way that the young men of our country view the issue. It may be a long process and a tough battle to win, but no change of this scale is ever easy.

The Schools

The curricula in our schools is largely dictated by politicians, be they members of the school boards or members of the President's Council on Education.

The No Child Left Behind Act has been central to American education, but it has led to a focus only on standardized testing and has done little to address the educational gaps we have when it comes to teaching life's pragmatic lessons. Legislators have the power to change the way children learn, and that can include learning about fatherhood if we choose to make it a priority.

Students in our country are taught courses they are not going to use, considering what many of them will be doing in the future. This waste of time begins in elementary school and continues through high school. It has created a void for real-world education, and there has always been a historical reality that the education system has never addressed: marriage and parenthood, two things that most people are going to experience at some time in their lives.

If the system required credit courses (more complex at different levels and more complete in high school) on marriage and parenting, we could in some way manage the effects of fatherless families and eventually lower their number. Many fatherless children would be given an understanding of what they've missed out on and perhaps avoid negative behaviors.

There has been a great deal of strife and argument over the ways we teach our children about sexuality. Lawmakers have fought over money for sex education that either focused or didn't focus on abstinence. They have pushed for campaigns that keep hormonally charged teenagers from having sex (unsuccessfully, I might add). But why aren't we teaching children about what happens after they have sex that results in the creation of life?

Some school systems have programs designed to scare children away from having kids while the students are still teenagers. These programs provide realistic baby dolls to teenagers in the hopes that once they see how difficult parenting is, they will have protected sex, or better yet, delay having sex until they are much older.

But what message do these programs send? Teenagers are likely to have sex whether we tell them to or not. And by providing them with a child, or even a "practice" one, and then portraying that child as being a negative consequence, we are raising a generation of children who have either no formal parenting education or one that emphasizes all the perceived negatives of parenting a newborn.

Either our teens know nothing about changing diapers, paying for a family, and supporting a mother, or they think that children are annoying—a price to be paid for a stupid mistake. We are all wrong in the ways we teach our students about parenthood.

It is imperative that we begin teaching our children the importance of parenting and the amazing experience that it really is when it is handled well, and when it is delayed until real adulthood.

We should begin in elementary school, well before we begin sex education. We could have classes that focus on parenting in general, but more specifically on fatherhood and what it means. If the young men in our schools really knew what fatherhood involved and the role they should play as fathers, perhaps fewer men would grow up and decide to have unprotected sex. Perhaps more men would decide to take an active role in the lives of the children that they decide to have.

The need to solve these problems exposes a general lack of practical education in our schools. For example, how many kids leave high school knowing how to balance a checkbook or what a mortgage really is? How many know how to rent an apartment or how to manage debt? Why aren't we teaching our kids the realities of everyday living? And why couldn't we include curriculum that explores the most important thing most people will do in their lives: creating children?

The curriculum does not need to be extensive or complicated. The basics of holding a baby, changing a diaper, preparing a bottle, and so on. By showing young men the everyday reality of fatherhood—its stresses, its rewards, its chores—we can better instill a sense of responsibility.

Young men rarely know the work that goes into being a mother, for example. By giving these young men a glimpse into a "day in the life" of a typical single mother, educators have the opportunity to show young men what they are doing to the families they might leave behind.

Many of the young men in our society are already the product of single mothers. You would think this circumstance would lead them to believe strongly in the responsibilities of a father, and in some cases it does. In many others, however, it has only the effect of making them believe a mother can do just fine on her own.

Taking a Stand on Sex

Our girls must take a stand.

By learning to take a stand early, they can build the self-esteem they will need later in life when they decide to have children. They will know how a responsible man acts and will have a good idea of what they are looking for in a husband and father. If their current boyfriend doesn't want to act responsibly, they will know that he is not going to be good material for a family.

Society must change in order to break the cycle of fatherless families. With a renewed focus on educating men about fatherhood and a push by women to get their spouses involved, we can begin the process of restoring the family unit.

The Lesson

When families have problems with their children, they usually complain about lack of government resources and alternatives to deal with the youth. I do not agree. That is making the government responsible for raising your child. Parents have to do their job. They did not ask the government's permission to make the baby.

However, there is one truth I am for. If we want to contribute to reducing crime and millions of negative situations caused by the disintegration of the first social unit, the family, we have to access young people where they are a captive market: in schools. If we all know they will someday be husbands, wives, fathers, and mothers, the curriculum has to get real.

Chapter **10**

DO'S AND DON'TS FOR FATHERS

There is no secret formula for being a great father. Each father's children will present unique gifts and unique challenges as the years pass. That's the beauty of being a father to your children; you get to see them grow as people. And if you're involved as you should be, you'll play a major part in molding the kind of people they become. In fact, you'll play a part in whom they become whether you're there or not; the difference, of course, is that if you aren't there for your children, you will negatively influence them as people, and I assure you that this will backfire.

There are, however, some do's and don'ts that all fathers should heed as they learn how to raise their children. And never forget that it is a learning process. You will most definitely not be ready to raise your children the day they come home from the hospital. It is an arduous and very individualized experience, even different from one child to another. You'll make mistakes, and there will be tense moments as you worry about your parenting. With perseverance, however, you can become a great father. As long as you start with a commitment to being involved in the lives of your children and wife, you will learn the rest.

Pay attention to these dos and don'ts, and you'll be ahead of the game:

Do: Attend the prebirth courses you are offered. Become an eager learner, ask questions, get involved.

Do: Read books and magazines about what to do when raising kids, especially when they are newborns. Although you will be living a hectic life, a simple, practical book for consultation can do a lot for you.

Do: Observe your child from his or her birth. Getting to know his or her reactions to every situation and to different foods and drinks will put you on the path to knowing what to do for that child in almost every scenario.

Do: Stay away from the old concept that newborns and babies may be spoiled if they are handled too much. The only love that babies understand comes through physical contact. They need it to grow and to face this cold world. Keep in mind that there will come a time when he or she is going to push you away and claim his or her independence.

Do: Ask the pediatrician all types of questions. But always keep in mind that your pediatrician sees your child once a month, while you live with your baby 24/7. If something happens that upsets you, call your doctor.

Do: See your baby as an individual. He or she does not have to do things at the same time nor in the same way as your friends' babies do.

Do: Remember that some things you learn will work for your baby, and some will not.

Do: Make yourself known at day care and school. Take an interest in the staff and teachers. Share with other parents and, from early childhood, get to know your child's friends and acquaintances. By the way, whenever your working hours allow it, go to special parties at school.

Do: Be available and ready to be with your children. It is not only about what nowadays is called "quality time" meaning that "quality" is more important than "quantity time". Don't fool yourself. You can't decide when your children will first walk or what their first words will be. You can't predetermine when your children will need to talk to you or what they might say. Being there for your children include "quantity" of time, so they know they can count on you.

Do: Be there emotionally for them. If you establish a good, trusting relationship when they are little, they will hear you when they grow old. Your children need to feel the freedom to talk to you about any issue, because your guidance is more important than you can ever know. They look up to you; you are the man they will try to emulate if they are boys, and the man they will try to find in a husband if they are girls.

In some stages of life, children seem not to listen to you. That is frustrating, but do not feel discouraged. They pretend to know more than you do, criticize you and even get nasty. However, national research on alcoholism and drug addiction has consistently revealed that the most influential people in the lives of young people ages thirteen through nineteen are parents. Parents' opinions are the most important to children, and so is their approval.

Do: Be ready to have a child and decide that you are committed to the process. That commitment manifests itself during pregnancy. Be at the doctor's appointments with your wife as she goes through pregnancy. Be there at the birth. Change the diapers. Prepare the bottles. Being present in the lives of your children is worth more than any gift you can give them or any house you can provide for them.

Do: Try to learn from your children's mother. Women are not born good mothers, even though most women have an instinctual ability to care for a child, but they do have an advantage. As life bearers, they have nine months to become physiologically and emotionally ready for motherhood. However, they are taught how to be (or not to be) good mothers by experience. Girls are given the responsibility of caring for younger relatives at parties, reunions, and other family gatherings. They are trusted as babysitters and are the immediate choice for helping take care of younger children when a caretaker is needed.

Boys, however, are not given these responsibilities as frequently as girls are. Boys are generally the ones being cared for as youngsters. They are the ones off playing with other boys as the girls babysit. So who do you think is better trained for raising children as adults?

The problem is that wives are not taught how to impart their wisdom to their husbands. Many women believe that men are supposed to be clumsy with babies and that, when a baby gets too fussy, they should take him or her away from Dad. This is a traditional mentality, and any father who automatically gives children back to Mother when they get fussy or won't stop crying has bought into it.

Raising children together is a partnership, and in a true partnership, there is no room for ego. If Dad doesn't know something, he has every right to his lack of knowledge, as does Mom. And if Mom sees that Dad is doing something wrong, she should gently show him how to do it right. But she shouldn't be quick to take the baby out of his arms, even if the baby is crying.

Men are just as capable as women of taking care of a child. They can be gentle and understanding. A man feels more bonded with his child when he's involved in the day-to-day care. Changing diapers is nobody's idea of fun, but it is a part of parenting.

Parenting in its truest sense is about providing for another human being. It is about selflessness and compassion. Sacrificing time with your friends or perhaps even a favored hobby in order to change those diapers is a path toward personal growth. You can learn a lot from giving your time to care for your children, and it will make you a better person.

Learning from one's spouse is also a great way for a couple to become closer. There will inevitably be moments of frustration during this process, and that's okay. Parenting isn't all roses and happiness. But if you and your partner can work together to take care of your children, you will learn how to transfer that communication and teamwork to other areas of life. Dealing with financial problems or family problems will become easier if you can learn how to share responsibility and to trust one another.

Do: Pass on good behaviors to your children. Some parents are part of the "do as I say, not as I do" crowd. They think that just by telling their children to avoid their own mistakes, they have done their jobs. Then they are shocked when their children act just as the parents do.

Please do not become a "do as I say, not as I do" father. Children learn behavior through modeling, not from words. You are not going to beat hundreds of years of research.

Your children watch you closely. They watch you every day. That's why children end up walking like their parents and talking like their parents. If you've ever known someone and their parents well, you have seen even small mannerisms that have been passed down: the way a father rubs his chin when deep in thought, or the way a mom plays with her hair when she's entrenched in a good conversation. The parents pass their behaviors down to their children.

You yourself have the mannerisms of the people who raised you, and you yourself have to make the decision to try to pass on the good ones to your children. If you have bad habits prior to having children, then make a conscious decision to eliminate at least some of them. This effort will go a long way toward keeping your children from picking them up.

Even in past decades, when a father held sway over his family and was revered as the head of household, he couldn't control the implanting of his behaviors in his children. Mimicking is central to how all animals learn to survive, as any nature show can tell you. The female polar bear shows her cubs how to hunt and how to fight. Humans are no different in some ways, but they are very different in others.

Animals that depend on instinct entirely for their behaviors do not have *intention* at their disposal; they simply do whatever they need to do to survive that day. We human beings, however, have much more choice. We can decide what we're going to do on any day and what behaviors we'll embrace. But those choices are made harder when we're raised by parents who exhibit negative behaviors.

You don't have to be a saint, but try to be the person you want your children to become. They'll learn from your example, and you'll be pleasantly surprised by how willing they are to adopt your positive behaviors.

Which brings us to our next item, a list of "dont's."

Don't: Assume that providing money is enough. There is a tremendous, natural instinct for men to provide for their families. Traditionally, men were hunters, and women tended to the children and were gatherers and farmers. These traditions have been passed down through time and have shown up in modern times as the belief that the man earns the money and the woman stays home with the children.

This system has largely evaporated in recent years as women have asserted themselves in the workplace to the betterment of everyone. Women are enjoying fulfilling careers and providing financially for their families in ways thought impossible just seventy years ago. But many men still feel it is their responsibility to provide financially for their children.

Money is important. Everyone who has ever had to pay a bill will tell you that. But money is not everything, and it certainly is no substitute for actual participation in raising your children. Some husbands believe that if they provide a nice house and a nice car for their wives, the wives should do the rest. After all, a woman is perfectly capable of raising a child on her own, right? Right, but it is not the best option. It is only half the deal. Fathers have to be there.

When you do not assume your role, your children will begin to perceive you as an absentee father, a walking ATM who doles out money in the place of real affection and love. After a while, your children will grow bored with new gifts because they will realize that those gifts cannot provide the emotional connection they seek.

A hug, a smile, a held hand—these things are worth more than all the gold in the world. Acknowledgment is an extremely powerful thing, and these small gestures provide it to your children. Think about your life and the lives of the people around you. The craving for acceptance and acknowledgment never goes away. People seek it their whole lives, but especially when they are children.

It's not uncommon to see a child saying over and over again, "Momma, Momma, Momma," until Momma turns to acknowledge him or her. In some cases, the child is trying to assert control and might be acting spoiled, but it is indicative of a basic need that children have: to be paid attention to.

Because of the cost of living today, many parents are forced to work multiple jobs, and in many cases, both parents have to work. This makes spending time with kids even harder. Some men work multiple jobs just to get by. That's admirable and sometimes necessary. Just make sure to provide the small gestures that show your children that you're paying attention. Frame one of their hand paintings and take it to work to put on your desk. Call them from work if you can to say good night. One way or another, find some way to be in their lives.

Maybe your concept of being a good provider or your dreams include striving for a better financial life, a bigger home, and making sure you have money for your children's college education. That is great. Just remember that, along the way, money is only one way of providing the pleasures of life to your family. Do not pretend to replace yourself with finances. Spend less time chasing money and more time chasing your kids.

Don't: Think you can be a father from afar. While some men are stuck at work and always wishing that they could be at home, others are far away from their children even when they have the option of being close. Relationships dissolve; it's a part of life. But many men assume that once a relationship is over, it's okay to move away from their families.

It is *not* okay to move away from your children. No matter how vindictive a relationship you may have had with your children's mother, your kids still need you there. No amount of phone calls, birthday cards, e-mails, and text messages will make up for your kids not being able to see your face and hear your voice in person.

Modern technology *has* made communication easier, but it hasn't necessarily made it better. Yes, you can send a live streaming video from anywhere in the world, but is that the same as playing in the backyard with your children? Probably not, but it is a nice try.

And this message isn't just for divorced dads. Many of you dads spend time traveling for business. Just keep in mind that you are sacrificing valuable time with your children. If you can, find a balance between work and home. Have you considered the possibility of working remotely from home?

Don't: Think that you can opt out of fatherhood. What would you do if the relationship with the mother of your children didn't work out? Have you thought about that? Do you know how you would handle it?

Some men believe that their relationships with their children are tied directly to the relationship they have with the children's mother. Some men think that if the relationship with a mom doesn't work out, they can sever ties with the kids, as if she and the kids are a package deal.

Well, the kids and the mother *are* a package deal in many ways, but that doesn't mean that you can abandon your children because you're mad at Mom. The kids didn't decide which home to be born into. They have no control over the way their father and mother act. All they know is that they need love and attention and that they want Dad in their lives. Make sure you remember that the next time you think about walking out the door for good.

The Lesson

If you think fatherhood is a burden and oh so complicated, you may be right. If you are asking yourself if your life after fatherhood will ever be like it used to be, the answer is *never*. After you become a father, you better turn the page on everything that went before. There is a B.C. (Before Child), and there is an A.C. (After Child). You have the huge responsibility of behaving properly so that you do not create a bad clone of yourself. Look at it this way: If you do a good job at that, it means that you are behaving well yourself.

A father-child relationship is forever. If your child grows up and has to live at the other end of the world, he or she is still your child. If you behaved like a father, distance will not damage the relationship. Although parenthood is intermingled with marriage, keep your parental role apart if something happens.

Chapter 11

DO'S AND DON'TS FOR MOTHERS

The role of mothers in supporting daddy to be a diligent, involved father in every way, is highly influential. When we have a partner who is more than willing to fulfill his parental role, we must embrace that feeling, and share our parenthood with a loving attitude. Anyway, even when society tells us so, we mothers do not become experts in child care from the moment our children are born. Let's share some do's and don'ts, for the sake of a happy family life.

Do have patience with your husband, even when he makes mistakes when fathering (assuming that such mistakes are not a danger to your child's well-being).

Yes, dads can be clumsy their first day on the job. As you read in the previous chapter, boys are not encouraged to take on the role of parent or caregiver early in their lives. They are taught to be tough and independent and to not show emotion. Well, being a new dad strips them of that independence and toughness. They are vulnerable and scared, and they need to be reassured that making reasonable mistakes is okay.

Do include your family in the education of your husband, but set the boundaries in advance. Teaching your husband how to be a good father is not a task that you have to do all by yourself. Your relatives could play an active role in helping you teach your husband about parenting. However, do not allow inappropriate interventions of family in paternal behavior or demeaning criticisms of it.

Your family should not be overbearing or controlling in teaching your husband, and you must make certain to prevent this from happening. Your husband must always feel important and needed in the process. He should not be made to feel like a child.

Men are prideful creatures. They take their manhood seriously, and molding them into diaper-changing fathers can take some time. That is why choosing a man who has the qualities of a good father is so important as you search for a lifelong partner. He must have the basic beliefs that support and endorse good parenting. You will learn about his relationships with his own family and his sense of responsibility in other areas of life when you are dating, as well as the important future issues that should be discussed before getting serious in a relationship, as I mentioned before.

If your husband is unwilling to learn from others, including the pediatrician, this might be a sign that he is unwilling to grow as a husband and a father. Perhaps you need a different strategy to approach him. Whatever the situation, don't give up on him.

Do allow your husband to create his own independent relationship with your children. As a unique human being, he has a different way of relating. As long as you both agree on the basics of raising children, allow and foster his creative ways. I learned to my surprise that girls take their ideas of active life and outdoor living from their fathers and not their mothers. Just think of how powerful fatherly input is when they establish their own bond their own way.

Do remember always that the daddy and your children are your partners in the life enterprise that is your family. Make sure that you plan meetings to discuss present and future finances, family trips, family days, Daddy's days with children, and Mommy's days with children. Good, enjoyable life, in spite of all the burdens and pressures we all have, is about *balance.*

Do erase from your vocabulary the phrase "wait until your father gets here" when your children misbehave. Using this phrase is one of the most damaging things you can do to your children and to you. Why?

You are showing your children that you lack the authority to correct misbehavior by yourself. If you do not have authority, why should they respect you?

You are also violating an important principle of teaching the relationship between certain behaviors and their consequences. When misbehavior happens, you have to apply the consequence immediately so that the child establishes the relationship between what he or she did and the consequence it brings. If disciplinary measures are delayed, children's minds cannot establish the relationship, and the discipline might be futile. I want to stress that I am not talking about physical discipline; I have a chapter ahead on that theme.

Lastly, you are injecting fear and anxiety into the father-child relationship, which could permanently damage it.

And, by the way, it is enough to take one disciplinary measure. When your husband comes home, you privately tell him what happened and what you did, but he does not need to punish them again.

As children grow older, parents have to find different ways of dealing with misbehavior based on its severity, but by that time, decisions must be made as a team, assuming the father-mother relationship is solid enough.

Do work on your couple relationship. The development and the well-being of a couple's relationship is the responsibility of both partners. However, there is an area of complaint many counselors hear about, one that is also frequently brought up on TV and radio in every culture: marital sex. It is incredible to hear about couples who have not had sex in weeks or even months. I ask myself, are they roommates or marriage partners? The fact that they have to take care of children is often their excuse, but the children then carry an unreasonable burden.

Yes, when children are newborns, it is tough for the parents to make time for sex. But couples tend to forget that they continually looked for opportunities for sex when they were dating. Is it really about the children? Is it about lack of interest? Or is it just easier to say no?

I have heard many young women tell me that "everything is not about sex; there are more important things in a marriage." Yes, sure—tell that to your husband. Finances, communication, sharing social interests, cooking—all of these "more important" things are indeed major concerns of any marriage. But just remember that the man's mind-set is different from yours.

I will never forget the college professor from whom I took a course in abnormal psychology. He was wise and brilliant and a very well-known and highly respected professional. When we were studying a chapter on marriage and couples relationships, he said, "Sex is the measure of communication and wellness in a marriage. If sex is unsatisfying, it permeates negatively into all the other means of communication in a very subtle way. When sex is satisfactory, disagreements are much more manageable. Of course, this mechanism is imperceptible to the human conscience."

Don't seek a partner who is a "father" to you. You need someone who will be a spouse to you and a father to your children.

As explained earlier in the book, women raised without fathers tend to look for a replacement for the rest of their lives, especially when selecting a husband. They look for the authoritarian figure who will tell them what to do and/or the protective figure who does everything for them. This is a recipe for disaster.

A woman needs a partner. If you were raised without a father, then understand that you can never replace his presence in your life through a surrogate. Your childhood was lessened if you were abandoned by your father, but that does not make you less of a person. You can raise your children with the help of a caring partner, someone who is an equal.

A good father does not seek to control his spouse or to make all the decisions. He understands that, as a partner, he must seek the counsel of his wife. He understands that her insight and knowledge are to be respected and incorporated into his own beliefs.

You won't be doing your child any favors by finding a father figure for yourself. If your spouse is absent as a spouse and a father, your children will miss out on the same things you so desperately craved yourself. I cannot stress enough that you keep this in mind while selecting a partner to share your life with: Choose a husband for you and a competent father for your children. You are going to need someone who is both.

Don't try to do it all. Stop the Supermom syndrome. If you are a controlling person, let go. Doing so will pay you great dividends. The laws of nature don't lie. You cannot be in two places at once even if you want to be. Because you can't be in two places at once, the father plays a crucial role in the whole process of providing children with the best possible upbringing.

Two heads are better than one, as the saying goes, and given the taxing nature of raising children, the saying holds true. You don't have to do it all in order to be a "model" mom. If you took seriously the images on the covers of women's magazines, you'd think that all women walk out of their homes in the morning looking spectacular in the latest fashions, hop into fashionable cars, drive to high-powered positions at work, and then return home to cook dinner, tutor their kids, and make love to their husbands.

Wake up! You don't find real women on magazine covers. Real women are not endowed with endless reserves of energy and enthusiasm; real women ask for help. It's okay to take time off work or to forgo that position on the PTA if you want to spend that time with your kids instead. And it's also okay to get away from the kids for a while.

Being empowered and intelligent and independent does not mean shunning help or the traditional household model. You are not less of a woman if you decide to be a stay-at-home mom. You are not less of a woman because you don't think you can handle raising your children and being engaged in a career.

Do not become your children's spokesperson with their father. That interferes with children-father communication. Your children, after a certain age, can speak for themselves loud and clear. If they have something to tell Daddy, they should tell him themselves. Of course, this presumes that Daddy has already learned to listen without overreacting.

This does not mean that you don't have a word about whatever they say. You do. But there is a moment when your husband and you discuss children's matters and come to agreements.

The Lesson

The first reaction we tend to have when a man is clumsy changing a diaper or feeding a child is to take the job out of his hands. If you get anxious or scared, watch over him until he learns. Don't say, "I'll do it," or, "Oh, you just don't know." You may lose the opportunity to teach your closest resource how to help you. Remember that only God is almighty, omnipresent, and omnipotent (although you want to think you are). You may feel that it's easier or faster to do things yourself, but do you really want to take all that burden on alone?

Chapter 12

LEGAL ENFORCEMENT

Legally enforcing good parenting is impossible, but that doesn't mean the law can't play a role in encouraging (or forcing, when circumstances allow) men to play a more supportive and active role in the lives of their children. The law can also act preemptively to encourage men and women to learn more about parenting prior to their decision to start families.

Before looking at what our courts *should* be doing, however, let's look at what courts and legislators are *currently* doing. Laws regarding paternal responsibilities vary from one state to another, and so do laws on marital rights and responsibilities, so passing a universal law regarding parental responsibilities might help develop a united front in a legal sense. But that's not the only problem with the current system.

One of the major problems we have in the system we use to enforce financial support is the idea that a child ceases needing support at the age of eighteen. Eighteen is actually the age at which many children need the most support in a financial sense (e.g., college), but most men think that their children really can make a decent life with only a high school diploma. A father has to ask himself, *Where were you when you were eighteen? Were you mature enough to understand that a better education will lead to a better, happier family?* At eighteen, children think they know life, but they need guidance and financial help to get a good education that gets them through in life. There are fathers who often spend more money on attorneys (so they can pay the amount of child support they want, whenever they want) than on their children. The judicial system helps them in a way because it has to abide with the law of the land that states that you are legally an adult at the age of eighteen.

And as soon as a child is eighteen (to me, an age at which children are still completely incapable of leading their own lives), the father cannot even ask medical questions about him. In most states, when a child turns eighteen, the court ceases all parental responsibility geared toward helping the child get into college or pursue any other endeavor. That leaves us with a bunch of immature and uneducated kids with limited skills who try to survive by taking any job they can find. Many of them are college material.

The sad truth is that our courts would be deemed hypocritical were they to try eighteen-year-old criminals as adults but then require that fathers support their children beyond this age. But it wouldn't be hypocritical at all. It makes perfect sense to support a law-abiding, hard-working good student until he is done with college. That does not contradict the issue of making an eighteen-year-old criminal be held responsible for his crimes.

Another problem we face from a legal standpoint is that, even when a father provides financially for children after they leave home, no law compels the father to see his children or to establish good relationships with them. A father's visitation rights are granted by law, and the mother has to abide by those visitation rights. But children have no recognized right under our current system to claim from a father the time they have lost. They cannot compel him to honor those visitations. As judges say, "The law cannot compel anybody to love anybody."

If the father is at home but is nonetheless an absentee parent, no law requires that he change his ways and start fulfilling his role as a parent. If a father doesn't want to be in the lives of his children, then he is going to be an absentee father.

And even though the law does play a role in assigning financial responsibility to a father, many jurisdictions do not live up to their responsibility of enforcement. The courts are supposed to support mothers in their fights for adequate support following most divorce proceedings or when a common-law marriage falls apart, but if the mothers' resources are limited, the job is difficult, and many mothers end up fending for themselves.

So how do we improve the legal system to make parenting a little better? Can we make changes at a legislative level that encourage not just financial compliance but also material involvement of fathers in the lives of their children?

The answer is a complicated one; the answer is both "yes" and "no." We can make changes at the legislative level that help prevent bad parenting, but we may never be able to force current fathers to *want* to be involved with their kids.

It may seem absurd to contemplate the idea of legislating fatherhood. After all, most of us want the government out of our lives as much as possible. And how would we create laws to make men better fathers even if we wanted to do so? Are these changes limited to just the financial and visitation aspects of divorce and separation? What can we do to enact the preventive measures our society needs to fix our national epidemic?

Change the Law

The way our laws are set up now, many divorced fathers think that their children are burdens to be off-loaded at the age of eighteen. And while we can't make these fathers view their children as the gifts they really are, we can emphasize lifelong involvement. Changes can be made to improve the support men provide their children even if they are absentee fathers. These changes could require financial support (including education and medical coverage) for children older than eighteen and require engaged couples and even divorced parents to take parenting courses so that they better understand how to handle the transition into or out of marriage.

The benefits of government involvement would outweigh the inefficient and lumbering way it sometimes operates. There would be real cost savings if these curriculum changes were effective. Think about the hundreds of millions of dollars spent on welfare, WIC (Woman Infant Child), and myriad other programs to support single moms. If we could convince our young men to take responsibility for the children they father, we would have homes that were more stable and more financially sound.

While many absentee fathers are not married to the mothers of their children, many others are. This provides an opportunity for an interdiction of sorts. Every married couple has to apply for a marriage license, and some states require that couples undergo blood tests to check for things such as HIV and AIDS. These prescreenings provide an excellent opportunity for the state to step up its requirements for a marriage license.

The state asks engaged couples to obtain a marriage license, but it doesn't ask these young couples if they have any experience caring for children or if they will be able to provide a good home to a child should they decide to conceive.

Because of modern liabilities, the federal and local governments are so afraid of getting into anyone's business or of seeming bigoted that they don't bother to say, "You need parenting lessons." A good way to avoid appearing discriminatory is to not discriminate. Anyway, this is a problem for everybody. No matter the financial situation of an engaged couple, the future mother and father should have to attend parenting classes.

It may seem like parenting classes run by the state would end up being just one more dysfunctional government program, but the benefits could far outweigh any inconvenience to the couples forced to take the classes. These costs would likely be offset if these potential new parents learned how to raise children the right way. After all, it's been shown time and again that children whose parents were not involved in their upbringing are far more likely to be involved in crime and other negative activities that cost our states millions of dollars.

The classes I'm proposing don't have to be complex, and they could be augmented by the classes I've proposed for our schools. In fact, they would almost certainly have to be part of a larger program of education in order to be effective.

It seems to me that just one approach to the problem of absentee fathers won't be sufficient. In order to really change attitudes on a national level, we would need a concerted effort by multiple organizations at multiple levels in order to get the message into the public consciousness.

But back to the classes. These classes could include some of the basics of parenting, such as diaper changing and bottle feeding, but they could also take advantage of the slightly older audience we would have in the form of engaged couples. These adults would hopefully be more mature than the kids in our high schools, and we could use that fact to talk to them about some of the intangibles of parenting that a younger audience might not be able to understand.

Parenting is difficult; there are just no two ways about that. Raising a child will challenge every fiber of your being on some days, but it will delight you beyond your wildest dreams on others. Through it all, it helps to understand what role you are to play as a parent and the incredible amount of influence you have over how your child develops.

If we can convey such a message to our newlyweds, we might have a chance to affect the quality, and therefore the outcomes, of their parenting. It might seem impossible to "give" someone patience, but if a couple at least knows what's coming, they will have a better chance of remaining patient through it all.

Again, the changes this effort makes may not be significant, but again, these classes would be only part of a larger program targeted at educating our future fathers and mothers about parenting. These classes could focus on patience, on mentoring, and on scheduling. They would teach the ways children respond to negative and positive reinforcement and demonstrate proven techniques that parents can use to help build their children's self-esteem.

The absolute necessity of patience would be one of the more important messages taught, because many parents give up on being involved when they feel frustrated or when they don't know what to do. This is especially true if they are young and have no real guidance or help from their own parents. The expression "it takes a village" is actually true, and all of our children would be better off if they had both parents and both sets of grandparents involved. The more love the better. In the absence of these neat "nuclear" families, though, the state has the opportunity to fill the vacuum.

Mentoring would also be an important part of the curriculum because many of our young parents don't understand that their jobs are not to be "cool" or to be friends with their children. Their jobs are to be mentors and to offer guidance and protection and wisdom. If you watch an infant with its parents, you'll see what I mean. A little girl, even just four months old, will watch every move her parents make. She will stare wide-eyed at the way they talk, eat, listen, move, and laugh. It's imperative that new parents know this and understand its implications. Someone who isn't a parent can't truly comprehend just how much children learn from their parents, especially in the early days of their lives. It's a tremendous responsibility and a tremendous blessing.

Scheduling is another area with which many young parents struggle. Life offers some strange and often abrupt changes in focus, and becoming a parent offers one of the strangest and most abrupt. By the time most people become parents, they have had a few years of living on their own and fending for themselves. This independence also comes with a certain amount of freedom, and that freedom is nice. It allows young men and women to go where they like and when they like. If they decide on the spur of the moment to go to a film late on a Friday night, they can. They simply grab their car keys and walk out the door.

The days of a single youth are focused solely on the wants and desires of that youth. Parenthood radically changes that focus, and the adjustment can be difficult to accept. One day a young man has the ability to determine his own schedule, and the next day his life is focused on an infant. Every trip, every errand, every day of work has to be vetted by the calendar of a very small human being. The inconvenience to parents who embrace this role is nothing in comparison to the overwhelming sense of love and affection that accompanies parenthood. It wouldn't hurt, though, to alert our newlyweds to this reality and to give them some time to think about how it will change their lives.

I'm confident that if more young couples knew the tremendous upside to parenting and the amazing benefits it offers in exchange for what amounts to trivial inconveniences, they would be more willing to embrace the role of parents. And they might be more inclined to put off the role until they are ready to accept the massive change in their lives that parenthood entails. After all, no matter how wonderful parenthood is, we don't want young couples feeling rushed into having children. We want parents to bring kids into this world when they are ready to play an active role in their lives, and not before.

If they gain insight into what parenthood demands and then decide not to have children because it is not their calling, they would be making a wise and mature decision.

Obviously, sending young, engaged couples to classes will not force all young men to accept the responsibility that being a father entails. We know that many, many kids are born out of wedlock, and this means that the parents of these babies never even registered for a marriage license. But that doesn't mean we shouldn't cover our bases and engage people where we can.

Following Through

Unfortunately, many men view their children as more of a financial burden than a blessing and gift. And while it's sometimes frustrating to deal with children and their decisions, this is no excuse for considering them a burden. This attitude comes from many sources, but in many ways it is perpetuated by the state and its laws.

As we discussed earlier in the book, the "it's yours for eighteen years" attitude many men have toward parenting is a result of how the government structures its laws toward financial responsibility and paternity. Men are required to provide financially even for children they didn't intend to have. This "obligation" is often seen as a short-term burden that can be cast off as soon as a child hits the age of legal adulthood. What a shame.

Why fathers believe that their children are capable of standing on their own once they turn eighteen is beyond me. Eighteen may be the age at which the government has decided a youth is old enough to fight and die in a war or to vote, but how many eighteen-year-olds do you know who have the life wisdom and the emotional maturity to guide themselves? It is an age of transition, and it is when children need their parents very much.

Our legislature can play a part in keeping fathers involved with their eighteen-year-olds, at least financially. Again, it is impossible to force a man to be caring and supportive. That's something he has to decide to be on his own. But the state can at least change the ways that child-support payments are made so that the age of adulthood, as seen by the family courts, is more like twenty-one.

Children's college education should be paid for until they finish even graduate studies, if they are students in good standing and not wasting time or money. Can you imagine how much money this change could save the nation in educational loans and grants?

Some people might argue against this move, saying that we cannot treat our eighteen-year-olds as adults in some arenas while at the same time treating them as still being the responsibility of their fathers in the financial arena. However, we already do this. We allow our eighteen-year-olds to vote, and we expect them to fight and die for their country, but we don't believe them responsible enough to control their alcohol intake. We make them wait until they are twenty-one before they can legally drink. Meanwhile, we expect them to support themselves and assume financially responsibility without realistic support.

So if we don't think that children under the age of twenty-one are responsible enough to even decide when they've had enough to drink, why do we think they're responsible enough to make life's major decisions or to support themselves financially with no assistance?

With the ever-growing costs of living in the United States, it has become commonplace for college graduates to move back with their parents. Few, if any, recent college graduates have enough earning power to purchase homes or even to pay rent for an apartment by themselves. Our family courts should have the right to determine, based on financial circumstances, what kind of support a father should give his children and whether he should be obligated to support or at least help his kids beyond the age of eighteen. Obviously, if a father is on welfare himself, it will be difficult to expect him to offer financial support, but even a little bit can go a long way.

The Payoff

So what would all of this government intervention get us? Would it spike our national and state budgets? Hardly. As stated before in this book, our governments already spend billions to support, educate, and—unfortunately—incarcerate the children of absentee fathers. It's an epidemic that will continue to cost us billions. Even worse, it will continue to produce children who are more likely to commit crimes or to be absentee parents themselves. We cannot sit idly by and watch as broken home after broken home goes unfixed. We must stand up and do something.

If even a few of these programs worked, our jails and youth centers would have fewer occupants and our nation as a whole would benefit beyond measure. Imagine the brainpower and the creativity wasted when our kids go down the path of crime and delinquency. These kids are lashing out because they feel unloved and unsupported, and the results are tragic. If we could keep these kids in school and away from crime, we could tap into their tremendous talents to enhance our culture and our workforce.

It would obviously be preferable for our families and communities to take the lead in pushing for better parenting.

Personal responsibility seems to have been lost a little bit in our country, and it seems that no one is willing to step up and say to their friends and relatives, "You should be doing better as a parent." It seems judgmental to us, and so it might be left to the government to step in and say it for us.

Chapter 13

REAPING REWARDS

Being a father is not easy. It's a lot of hard work, and it's a learning process. While most men try to project strength and toughness, the reality is that men are just as scared of parenting as women are; in fact, usually more so.

Many men are raised without direct experience of infants, and that lack of experience makes the transition to parenting even more difficult. Men need to be supported and coached, and they need a lot of positive reinforcement to help them become an accomplished parent and comfortable in the role.

Some mothers are more supportive than others when it comes to teaching their husbands how to do the "nuts-and-bolts" work of parenting. They give their husbands guidance in doing certain things, such as changing diapers, feeding the baby, and giving baths, but they allow room for their husbands to find their own way of doing things. This kind of support is necessary for helping a man learn how to watch a child on his own, but it isn't enough to turn him into Dad. That takes an approach that addresses his mental and emotional state, which we'll talk about throughout this chapter.

Unfortunately, many women don't understand how fragile their men are. They buy into the stoicism that some portray, or they mistake hesitance for disinterest. Other women are not as accepting of "someone else" taking care of their children. Unfortunately, this overprotective instinct can be strong enough to include the father, and many men are shut out of daily parenting as a result of this attitude.

This is a dangerous situation, because if the father is left out of taking care of his children, he can become distant from them and resentful of how much of the mother's time they consume. After all, the father was a partner to the mother first, and when he sees his place beside Mom being supplanted, he can't help but feel left out.

Some men aren't secure enough to move aside so that Mom can provide Baby with the needed love and support.

The way some men react to the arrival of a child is very much like the way older siblings react when a newborn is brought home; they will show anger or resentment toward the new addition to the family and even toward the mother who brought it home. Men see Mom lavishing attention on Baby and can't accept the loss of physical intimacy and emotional interaction they once shared more frequently with their partners.

The Need for Approval

People naturally crave approval, whether from parents, peers, or spouses. The questions are whether a man's need for approval interferes with his sense of self and whether he learns to share time and energy with his children. And how does a modern family balance individuality with the need for approval?

Let's be very real. The modern trend in religious and humanistic and psychological disciplines is to help people relinquish their need for approval and to help them move away from dependence on others for their self-esteem. Many people were raised with a psychopathic need for approval, which means they'll do anything to get it. They don't make rational decisions about how to act, and for a father, this can be tragic.

We naturally like approval, but we have to be able to live without it. These modern schools of thought are pushing people toward living their own lives regardless of whether their actions meet with the approval of those in their social and familial circles. In many ways, this is the right way to go.

We've all seen teenagers pushing themselves in one of two directions: toward the approval of their parents (sometimes at the expense of their own personal desires) or radically against the wishes of their parents. Thus, the push in modern circles to alleviate some of the pressure that adolescents and adults put on themselves. Some people view these extremes as being the result of an unhealthy reaction to the need for praise. Some teens don't believe they can win the approval of their parents, and so they lash out, trying desperately to get attention.

When it comes to grown-up teens, i.e., men, the need for approval is alive and well. Even if a man feels confident of himself and his abilities, he still wants to know from his wife and from his children that he is doing a good job. Many women are unsure how to handle "training" or supporting the father of their children, and they don't know how to give him this approval in a genuine way.

Many mothers think that their primary job is to train their children, and it is. But they should take time to help the fathers feel involved and supported in the raising of their children. It's critical that the fathers understand that they are *needed* in the partnership and that the health of their children depends on them.

Several types of positive reinforcement can be used to build the parenting confidence of a father. They address his self-esteem and confidence from the varying sources of love in his life, beginning with himself. This, of course, assumes that we are talking about men within a normal range of mental health.

Self-Approval

The first type of positive reinforcement comes from within. To achieve self-approval, a father has to "educate" himself, practice the role of parent, see the results of his "good job," and start developing his own standards of achievement. To accomplish this, he needs support, love, and recognition when he does well with his child. Dad will likely look to Mom for this support, and for the first few years of a child's life, he might look to Mom to decide whether he is doing his job well.

A good way to show your man that you trust him is to appeal to his nature. Parenting is really a craft, and men can relate to practicing a craft. If they are given a chance to get involved, get their hands dirty, and make some mistakes, they'll learn to enjoy the process. Some men are naturally competitive, and they want to get good at what they are doing. Give your man a chance, and you'll soon find him racing to see how fast he can change a diaper or trying out new ways of getting that "onesie" on his daughter so that she doesn't cry when it goes over her face.

Feeling Love and Acceptance from the Child

There is no feeling in the world like looking down at your newborn and seeing her or him look back up at you. There is nothing like it. The love that emanates from a new parent is usually unconditional, depending on the circumstances under which the child was born. Children are so pure and so free of cynicism and pessimism that one can't help but see joy in their arrival.

Children don't hold grudges. They make no judgments and demand no conditions on their acceptance of their parents. They want only to be loved and taken care of; that's all they ask. To newborns, their parents are perfect. They are Momma and Papa, people who have the ability to lift their spirits, to make them feel special and loved.

Unfortunately, some parents don't see this love right away. Some new parents think that a fussy or colicky baby is uncomfortable with them personally or prefers one parent over the other. They then project their feelings of disappointment and frustration onto the child, as though the child has consciously decided to ignore them or to cry in their arms. These feelings are dangerous because they can engender in a parent a sense of bitterness toward infants who have no choice in how they feel or when they cry.

Even babies who are pleasant don't always appear to some parents to be "loving" in the way the parents expected. The days and weeks following a child's birth are a very delicate time. Parents, especially new parents, are unsure of what to expect, and many of them feel vulnerable. They are now responsible for another human being but don't always know what to feel or what to say and do.

Some parents expect a euphoric period to follow the birth and aren't prepared for the exhaustion and stress that come from taking care of a newborn. For some of these parents, their lost expectations take the bloom off the rose. They feel as though the experience is somehow diminished, and they give up some of the connection to their children.

In some cases, there is a very real problem in the way parents feel following a birth. For some women, postpartum depression creates a numb feeling. In extreme cases, they feel nothing toward their children, and it can take time and medical treatment to help them overcome this challenge.

The situation is slightly different for men in that their biological systems aren't going as haywire, but it can still be difficult for them to build a bond.

This may seem unbelievable to parents who fall immediately in love with their children, but everyone handles parenting differently. The moment a child is born, the lives of both parents change forever. There is life before the child, and then there is life after. This transition, so sudden and so powerful, can affect a person's mental status.

To some men, the birth of a child is seen as the beginning of a lifelong burden because the child is the result of an "accident" or because his relationship with the mother is hostile or has fallen apart completely. Such men are blinded by anger and resentment, and so they ignore the obvious bond with the child. It's as though they want to distance themselves because admitting love for a child would be accepting the situation as "okay." It's a terrible way to treat a child.

Children are guiltless. They have no malice and no resentment. Their arrival into the middle of a conflict can negatively affect them for life because parents will project their anger and fear onto the child, as though the baby has done something wrong or has made the situation worse. For men like this, there is always the hope that seeing their child grow up will soften their hearts.

It's easy for new parents to get flustered and distracted by the overwhelming sense of responsibility. Mom, it's so important that you help Dad transition into fatherhood. Sometimes he'll need help to feel comfortable with his child. Helping him with this comfort can foster and nourish the love he feels from his child and move him closer toward embracing fatherhood.

The more time a father spends with his child, the more likely he is to feel a close bond develop between them. Children learn new things every day, and when a man sees his child laugh or crawl or walk for the first time, it helps him see how special his child is. When his child smiles at him and says "Dada" for the first time, he's almost certain to feel the pure love coming from his child.

Approval from Mom

Always remember that you and your husband or partner found a spark in each other before you had a child. Keep that in mind as you raise your baby, and try to find time to help Dad feel good about himself. As difficult as it may seem, find some time to work on the relationship with Dad.

The months following a birth can be extremely difficult both physically and mentally for a woman. There is little sleep to be had, and the responsibility of breastfeeding can add an extra challenge. In these months, Dad needs to know how you are feeling; if he thinks that you are ignoring him, he has to know that it is only because you have no more energy and focus to give.

Once those first months have gone by, make sure to rekindle the romance that led to Baby in the first place. It may take time to get comfortable with one another again, but intimacy is a big part of showing Dad that he's still important. And when it comes to helping him raise Baby, a steady stream of encouragement and approval will go a long way.

Raising a Good Person

Even among the frantic moments of child rearing, you must always keep priorities straight. Parents have a real job to do, and approval of that job should be contingent on real accomplishment.

Sometimes a dynamic develops between fathers and their children that is a result of the father being at work most of the day. In many families, the mother is the everyday "enforcer," making sure that the children are following rules are being disciplined when they don't. The father who comes home after a long day of work doesn't want his precious time with his kids to be stressful. He doesn't want to spend his time disciplining his children or being the "bad guy." Consequently, many men end up allowing their children to get away with things their spouses would stop.

The result of this dynamic is that the mother is made out to be the villain because she isn't the "softy" the father is. She puts her foot down and sets boundaries, whereas the father just wants to have fun. It is absolutely crucial that the father take an active role in helping to raise good people. It isn't enough that he's in the home or that he makes it back to the house in time for dinner. He must take an active role in setting boundaries for his children, even if that limits how much he can be their friend.

The opposite of this dynamic is the one where Mom sets Dad up as the enforcer, the "bad cop." She says to her kids, "You wait till Dad gets home! I'll tell him what you did." This is a major mistake in parenting in that it pits the father against his children. If a man is working full-time, he doesn't have very much interaction with his children, especially when they are very young and go to bed early. It isn't fair to use him as a sort of boogey man who will punish the children when he gets home.

Unfortunately, some parents don't feel comfortable disciplining their children, and so they project the role of disciplinarian onto the other parent. They convince the children that if they don't listen, the other parent will come home and do what they aren't willing to do. It's an abdication of responsibility that hurts not only the children but also the marriage. When one spouse feels as though he or she is being thrown under the bus, it creates distrust and suspicion. The parents begin to wonder why the children are afraid of them and whether they are doing something wrong.

For parents, the task of raising children to be good people comes right after protecting them. If a man doesn't understand the importance of what he is supposed to be teaching his children, he starts to believe that he should be "hands-off" and that he should let his children develop on their own and find their own personalities. And while parents need to give children independence and freedom, this particular pendulum can swing too far. A father can be too hands-off and can make his children feel as though there are no boundaries. When a child thinks that there are no boundaries, he or she can also feel that there is no parental involvement or love. Such kids keep pushing for some form of recognition and discipline and are often unruly. They simply want their parents to be involved.

Because a father plays such a significant role in the way his children perceive men in general, it's imperative that he act as he wants his children to act. If he wants them to be respectful, then he must act respectfully toward those around him. If he wants them to display temperance in their behavior, he too must show restraint.

Many parents believe that they will have done their jobs if they pass on just the "life lessons" they've learned. They simply don't realize how closely their children are watching them and how "cheap" words really are. Children will listen when you talk, but your words don't carry the same weight that your actions do.

It isn't up to Mom to keep Dad in line, but a little prodding and "training" doesn't hurt. If Mom reminds Dad of his influence on the kids and points out how much they look up to him, he might have an easier time making the connection between his own behavior and the behaviors his children will exhibit as adults. Of course, Dad will be much more aware if the Mom-Dad relationship is solid.

When a man does a good job of teaching his kids and shows them through example how he wants them to behave, Mom should commend him on his behavior. Every father likes to be told that he's doing a good job. Hearing Mom say, "I really appreciate the way you've been helping out," can go a long way toward keeping Dad's confidence and self-esteem high.

Giving Dad positive reinforcement isn't a matter of lying to him. A woman shouldn't tell her husband that he's doing a good job when he isn't. Positive reinforcement is about helping a man become a better father over time.

Parenting is a graduate school of sorts, except parents never finish their degrees. They just keep learning and keep learning and try their best to help their children become good people.

If a man can believe in himself and his abilities as a parent and then combine that belief with patience and perseverance, he'll be well on his way to becoming a great dad. And if he can see the love his child has for him, he'll know why he gets up at night, changes diapers, and puts up with the frustration of learning to be a dad. If his spouse supports him in this endeavor, he'll be a great dad.

Chapter 14

NO FATHER ON EARTH, NO FATHER IN HEAVEN

Ask yourself this question: If you cannot trust the biological father you can see and touch, how can you trust a Father you cannot see or touch or hear or smell, one you cannot perceive with your physical senses? If you don't have a father to look up to and who protects you, how are you going to believe there is a Higher Father or Being who supports you? More than that, if you have a punitive, intolerant, and condemning biological father, why would you need or want a punitive spiritual father?

No wonder a nation whose population is allegedly 75 percent Christian has such a crime rate. In a nation founded "under God," so many people deny God's existence, negotiate with it their own way, or never become active Christians. Thousands of people reject the concept of spirituality no matter the doctrine involved. The young population refuses to go to any church.

When we have an absentee father with everything implied in it, we cannot transfer the trust we usually put in a physical father, to a Father or Higher Being we cannot see with our physical eyes. The feelings of emptiness, loneliness and being out there by yourself with nobody to turn to are overwhelming, because we feel we have no father on Earth. How can we "buy" the idea of having a Father in Heaven?

Most infants and children do not acknowledge their spirituality, at least consciously. If their male role model (father) is absent in any way (physically or emotionally), they have no way to transfer the image to the spiritual being, or Father God. A

The absence of a father has another devastating impact in the life of a human being: It deprives him or her of any hope of developing the spiritual support system that everybody needs when situations get out of control. They end up not only lacking a father on Earth, but they also find it tough to accept and embrace a Father in heaven. Indeed, it is hard for them even to consider any concept of a higher spiritual being. Faith, which is the resource for endurance in any religion, is almost impossible to adopt.

If you have studied developments in civilization, you have learned that human beings habitually turn to a higher power and infinite intelligence for support, comfort, and hope whenever they do not have control over a situation.

Religion (meaning "reunion with a higher power") has been part of the belief system of a vast majority of civilizations for centuries. Even science has acknowledged its power of endurance through hardships in people's lives. For more than thirty years, renowned physicians like Larry Dorsey, Bernie Siegel, Herbert Benson, and Andrew Newberg—just to mention a few—and highly respected health institutions like Harvard, Johns Hopkins, the University of Pennsylvania, and many more have scientifically studied the effects of faith and spiritual life in health issues. Researchers of antiaging have included religious belief as one factor that influences longevity. Spiritual life is meaningful for surviving the hardships of corporeal life. Every religion and spiritual belief agrees with that. But how do you buy into that if what you live contradicts what you hear?

I respect all religions and belief systems, but the one I am most acquainted with is Christianity, so that is the one I will refer to in this chapter.

The Concepts of God

God is presented as a Father; indeed, the perfect Father. Different Christian denominations, according to emphasis on Full Gospel, New Testament, or Old Testament, describe Him in two main ways: as a protective, supporting, compassionate and guiding father with unconditional love who is always there for His children no matter what they do and fosters forgiveness and grace; or as a punishing, angry Father who fiercely disciplines us if we don't do what He says and fosters blame and guilt.

Sorry to say, many denominations sell out to the latter concept, and most children in our nation grow up with that concept. People transfer that particular father concept to the biological father figure and transfer the concept of a negative father figure to an invisible and intolerant father.

To worsen the picture, many "present" fathers follow that pattern of behavior toward their children because that is what they were taught. That leaves the human being with nobody to turn to, hopeless, fearful, and with a sense of guilt that is very hard to live with.

If you had an absent or abusive father, would you go to church to find the same spiritual Father? I don't think so, but it may happen. People who are negatively conditioned to this type of father as being "normal" will accept that punitive God as "right."

Other denominations, most of them inspired by the New Testament, introduce a Father God who is forgiving and understanding, someone who always grants a second chance. They do not perceive God as a punitive father but as one who gives free will, which comes down to two choices: doing the right thing or doing the wrong thing according to divine and natural laws. If your choices break any divine or natural laws, He has the compassion to forgive you, but you cannot avoid the consequences of your own behavior, and they are not His punishment. It is about taking responsibility for your decisions and actions. These denominations preach that you should embrace God out of love and not out of fear.

People react to both representations of God the same way they react to life, by making one of two choices. Either they go along with what they live and keep repeating the pattern because it is known to them, or they go exactly in the opposite direction. When there is no father at home or there is a punitive one, the person can become rebellious, deny the existence of God, or believe that there is a punishing God and stay away from Him and from church. Another person under the same circumstances may look for God as the Father he or she lacks at home and cling to Him as a support, a comforter, and a helper.

With all due respect, sometimes structured religion wants to exert an excessive control over the spiritual life of people, putting a stress on the Father-child spiritual relationship that makes life worse. As in human life with the natural father, people should be encouraged to develop their own intimate relationship with

God. In the same way that a child should not need a spokesperson between his natural father and himself, God's child should have a direct relationship with the spiritual Father and be inspired to develop a personal spiritual life.

Is Church fulfilling its role against absent fatherhood?

Churches of all denominations do their part of social work, which is very significant. They help the poor and the homeless, provide food and clothing, and develop different programs to alleviate the needs of certain groups in our communities. However, there is a high divorce rate among Christians, and more teen pregnancies, fatherless families, and single mothers than you might expect.

The same way I highly suggest an educational curriculum on fatherhood at school, it is time for Church to get real and attach itself to the Word in the Bible in a practical way. If they are going to preach a godly lifestyle, Church should attack the absentee father problem by educating the following groups:

- Young men: They are on time to do things right. Sow in them the right behavior toward themselves and toward women and develop a realistic view of creating a family. Remind them of the importance of being independent and of choosing a wife who is a life partner, not a servant or a slave or a housekeeper. Teach them about choosing a good partner, the value of education, finances, and the pride and responsibilities of fatherhood. After all, don't they have the best role model of a Father they can copy?
- Young women: Along with Biblical values, teach them realistic information about why it is not convenient for

them to have children out of wedlock or an unwanted pregnancy. Teach them to choose a right partner, because not every man who attends Church will make a good husband and father. Train her about what marriage is really about so she learns to make sound decisions.

- Men: Emphasize the need for them to be partners in their marriage, to get involved in their families, to be held accountable financially and emotionally for their children, and to get involved in fatherhood beyond any cultural belief they have that tells them otherwise.
- Women: There are more than 100 unforgettable women in the Bible—wise, intelligent, brave, defiant, good wives, and wonderful mothers. Teach women to use their wisdom to raise boys who stand on their own and girls who make good marriage choices. Teach them to dare to create a partnership with their husbands and help them into becoming participant fathers.

Churches can intervene with fatherless families in their congregations and address them in brave, wise ways so they can help reduce the impact of the problem in their community.

Chapter **15**

DISCIPLINE ISSUES

For centuries, structured religion, diverse cultural groups, and society as a whole have fostered, promoted, and condoned the physical punishment of children. I still hear well-educated people, including preachers, enticing parents, especially fathers, to use corporal punishment to discipline children, being proud of doing it themselves and denying with real conviction that they are violating the law and committing child abuse. Of course, these are the same people who raise their children in emotionally abusive ways. They have big trouble understanding the laws on child abuse and, unfortunately, they still have the blessing of people who couldn't care less about anything until it occurs in their own families.

Most of these fathers (women do abuse, but this book is devoted to fatherhood) still believe that they have unlimited power (as opposed to authority) over their children, even to harm them. There is a lot of incongruence going on here. You will notice that these men

- condemn child abuse.
- say you can hit but you cannot abuse, while they boast about threatening their children with beatings.

- talk about the importance of being a good role model. (Of what? Of hostile behavior, violence, and double standards?)
- say all the time that they would "kill" the guy who dares hit their daughter. (They do not mean that they would commit suicide.)
- boast about being intelligent and advanced in every field of knowledge. (Really?)
- blame modern times and modern psychology for children's and teens' behavior today.

Observe the children of fathers such as these. They are repressed, shy, scared, rebellious, aggressive, or violent. If they do not exhibit those traits today, wait until they grow up. For the sake of fathers who want to learn, let's share some realities:

- Neither psychology nor modern times are to blame for the incompetence of parents when it comes to discipline. I have never read a single psychology textbook or a popular book or attended a psychology course that taught me that children have to be left to do whatever they wanted. Child psychology tries to teach parents to discipline in the most effective and healthful ways to help a child develop as a social being.

  Children need and crave structure, routine, and discipline. When they do something wrong, they have to learn the consequences. Consequences not related to the wrongdoing are misdirected, as is physical punishment. People want easy fixes. It is easier to spank or hit than to take the time and effort to think of a response that imparts a lesson without doing harm and is proportionate to the fault. For some people, hitting a child is a good way to hit somebody who is not going to retaliate.

- Consider this damaging incongruence. A father hits a daughter and tells her, "This hurt me more than it hurt you, but I hit you because I love you." The message that he is sending and she is receiving is, "When a man loves you, he will hit you, but that's okay." Remember that he is the role model for men in her life and that his behavior sets the scene abusive relationships in her life.

- Every excessive force against an innocent person is abuse. There is no negotiating this.

- Those who try to handle situations with violence are really insecure about their authority. Those who are good role models and good examples earn the authority to talk their children out of wrongdoing. The children will respect them because the parents do what they say, and example speaks much louder than words.

  Society is packed with "Do what I say, not what I do" fathers. *That just doesn't work.* Be responsible enough to set a good example. Your children will respect your right and authority to tell them what to do.

  When talking doesn't work for them (it may happen), consider stopping a privilege for a while in proportion to age and behavior. Believe me, your children will learn the lesson and will think twice before repeating the behavior. When they grow up, they will remember you with love and pride and not with resentment.

- What is discipline? I bet most people relate *discipline* to punishment. The origin of the word *discipline* has to do with "making disciples." When you discipline your child, you should be instructing him. He or she is your disciple. Don't you expect your children's teachers to set examples for them? You should do the same for your children.

• Violence engenders violence, and so does aggressiveness. When you are violent toward your child, you are telling him that is the right way to react to situations. Maybe he would never be aggressive toward you, but he will discharge that ingrown aggressiveness toward his children, his wife, or whatever other relationships he has. Maybe you will even have to bail him out of jail.

You are the authority. You don't need to hit your child to prove it. If you set a good example, you will have your child's respect. Your voice and the proportionate removal of privileges will be enough discipline.

Yes, being a good father takes a lot of patience and wisdom. Nobody told you that it is easy to be a good father. But it pays.

Chapter 16

AN INVITATION

I must confess that, in this journey of becoming aware and creating awareness of the immeasurable impact of absent fathers on families and in societies throughout the world, I have felt frustrated by indifferent attitudes and by others' belief that this is just a "normal change in present society," as I have heard many times. It seems that when a behavior becomes general, we accept it as normal, even at the cost of unhappiness, lowered mental health, and severe consequences for people and society. We can add the attitude of "if it doesn't hurt me, I couldn't care less."

My hope lies in an emerging generation of men who get involved in fatherhood with passion, knowledge, and genuine interest and accept the challenge of raising children and all that it entails. I am also hopeful for the new generation of women who, although they know they are capable of being self-sufficient, promote and entice their husbands' involvement in raising the children even before they are born. Even more, they are very sensible when choosing their life partners.

This book revolves around the roots of absent fatherhood, and it proposes solutions at every level. However, I want to end with a letter addressed to Dad because Dad is the one who has to make the decision to change. As with any problem, small or large, we first have to admit the problem exists and then open ourselves to the options available to solve it.

Dear Dad,

Fatherhood is an issue of love and personal accomplishment. Today, maybe you see it as an unbearable responsibility, but as you embrace it with your heart, you will know what real manhood is.

That guy or girl you created in partnership in many ways is and will be a copy of you. Is there a better way of transcending one generation after another? There is no better opportunity than this to improve yourself and set an example, so you can feel proud when you look back on today.

I want you to know you can be as competent as anybody with changing diapers, looking after your children, playing with them, feeding them, helping with homework, and taking the time to really know them. You can be the best counselor of both son and daughter on love issues; the best role model for choosing the best partner for life. The show of appreciation and joy on their faces will be your very heartfelt reward.

Your reward will be greater with each of your child's life stages you put your efforts into, when you see them make decisions that bring you happiness and peace of mind.

REFERENCES

1. Bendheim-Thomas Center for Research on Child Wellbeing and Social Indicators Survey Center, 2010. *CPS Involvement in Families with Social Fathers.* Fragile Families Research Brief No.46. Princeton, NJ and New York, NY:

2. Bronte-Tinkew, J., Horowitz, A., & Scott, M. E. (2009). *Fathering with multiple partners: Links to children's well-being in early childhood.* Journal of Marriage and Family, 71, 608–631.

3. Bush, Mullis, and Mullis 2000. *Differences in Empathy Between Offender and Nonoffender Youth* https://www.ncjrs.gov/App/Publications/abstract.aspx?ID=184359

4. Carr and Spriner 2010. *Advances in Families and Health Research in the 21ˢᵗ Century.* http://onlinelibrary.wiley.com/doi/10.1111/j.1741-3737.2010.00728.x/abstract

5. Coley and Mediros 2007. Coley and Medeiros 2007. *Reciprocal Longitudinal Relations Between Nonresident Father Involvement and Adolescent Delinquency* http://onlinelibrary.wiley.com/doi/10.1111/j.1467-8624.2007.00989.x/abstract

6. Edin, K. & Kissane R. J. (2010). *Poverty and the American family: a decade in review.* Journal of Marriage and Family, 72, 460-479.

7. *www.fatherhood.org/the-father-factor*

8. *www.fatherhood.org/father-absence-statistics*
9. *fatherhoodfactor.com/us-fatherless-statistics*
10. *www.fathers.com › Statistics and Research*
11. www.fatherhood.org/the-father-factor
12. www.fatherhood.org/father-absence-statistics
13. fatherhoodfactor.com/us-fatherless-statistics
14. www.fathers.com › Statistics and Research
15. Guterman, N.B., Yookyong, L., Lee, S. J., Waldfogel, J., & Rathouz, P. J. (2009). *Fathers and maternal risk for physical child abuse.* Child Maltreatment, 14, 277-290.
16. Harper and McLanahan 2004. *Father Absence and Youth Incarceration.* http://onlinelibrary.wiley.com/doi/10.1111/j.1532-7795.2004.00079.x/abstract
17. Hoffmann, John P. *The Community Context of Family Structure and Adolescent Drug Use.* Journal of Marriage and Family 64 (May 2002): 314-330.
18. James, Doris, *Profile of Jail Inmates 2002*, http://www.bjs.gov/content/pub/pdf/pji02.pdf
19. Matthews, Curtin, and MacDorman 2000. *Infant Mortality Statistics from the 1998 Period Linked Birth/Infant Death Data Set* https://www.cdc.gov/nchs/data/nvsr/nvsr48/nvs48_12.pdf
20. National Fatherhood Initiative. *Family Structure, Father Closeness, & Drug Abuse.* Gaithersburg, MD: National Fatherhood Initiative, 2004: 20-22.
21. Nord, Christine Winquist, and Jerry West. *Fathers' and Mothers' Involvement in Their Children's Schools by Family Type and Resident Status.* (NCES 2001-032). Washington, D.C.: U.S. Department of Education, National Center for Education Statistics, 2001.

22. Osborne, C., & McLanahan, S. (2007). *Partnership instability and child well-being. Journal of Marriage and Family,* 69, 1065–1083.

23. Paulson, J.F., Keefe, H.A., & Leiferman, J. A. (2009). *Early parental depression and child language development.* Journal of Child Psychology and Psychiatry, 50, 254–262.

24. Quinlan, Robert J. *"Father absence, parental care, and female reproductive development."* Evolution and Human Behavior 24 (November 2003): 376-390.

25. Teachman, Jay D. *"The Childhood Living Arrangements of Children and the Characteristics of Their Marriages."* Journal of Family Issues 25 (January 2004): 86-111.

26. U.S. Census Bureau, *Children's Living Arrangements and Characteristics*: March 2011, Table C8. Washington D.C.: 2011.

ABOUT THE AUTHOR

Ofelia Perez has a background in psychology and was a journalist for more than thirty years. She is an author, professional writer, book researcher, book editor, and pastoral counselor. This is Perez's second book.

Made in the USA
Coppell, TX
12 June 2021